The
Essential Fromm

Life Between Having and Being

D0869614

· ERICH FROMM ·

The Essential Fromm

Life Between Having and Being

_____

Edited by R A I N E R   F U N K

• • •

Portions translated by

L A N C E   W.   G A R M E R

C O N T I N U U M   ·   N E W   Y O R K

2000

The Continuum Publishing Company
370 Lexington Avenue
New York, NY 10017

Copyright © 1993, 1995 by The Estate of Erich Fromm
Foreword and compilation Copyright © 1995 by Rainer Funk

Printed in the United States of America

Library of Congress Cataloging-in-Publication Data

Fromm, Erich
    [Selections. English. 1995]
    The essential Fromm : life between having and being / edited by
Rainer Funk ; portions translated by Lance W. Garmer.
        p.   cm.
    Includes bibliographical references (p.).
    ISBN 0-8264-1133-9 (paperback : alk. paper)
    1. Conduct of life. 2. Life. 3. Humanistic psychology.
I. Funk, Rainer.   II. Title.
BF637.C5F77213   1998
158—dc20   95-20445
                                                                CIP

Contents

Editor's Foreword

Our life is a "life *between* having and being." This is the experience of many people who are moved by Erich Fromm's alternative of "having or being" and who can be motivated to a change in their lives. Erich Fromm formulated the alternative in the book *To Have Or to Be?* in 1976. In 1989, nine years after Erich Fromm's death, this book was followed by another that bore the title *The Art of Being* (Continuum, 1992), which contained chapters from his posthumous writings that he had intended for the book published in 1976 but, for various reasons, did not publish at that time.

The alternative of "having or being" serves many people as a key to an understanding of what they value consciously, semiconsciously, or unconsciously and of what they actually pursue passionately in their lives. Not only does it allow one to understand conceptually and to diagnose what really goes on within each of us, but it is at the same time a viable guiding notion for changing our lives as well.

Whoever tries to discern his own orientation toward having and to practice an alternative with orientation toward being develops the need to learn even more about the path toward it. The present reader concerning the alternative of "having or being" hopes to meet this need. It does not seek to replace readings of the two books *To Have Or to Be?* and *The Art of Being,* but rather to complement them. This results from the selection of the texts collected here as well as from the manner of their compilation. Moreover, *The Essential Fromm: Life Between Having and Being* seeks to reduce the large number of misunderstandings surrounding the alternative of "having or being" and to pick out those aspects that, after a nearly twenty-year-long acquaintance with Fromm's alternative, have proven to be especially fruitful and instructive.

Much of what is formulated in well-chosen words in the two books mentioned makes an impact only in the form of the spoken word. Lectures and interviews are thus an important complement and addition. Erich Fromm did indeed write all his books in English, but, when *To Have Or to Be?* was being written during the 1970s, he gave a series of lectures in German and granted numerous German interviews. The transcripts of these interviews and lectures, which are otherwise inaccessible or accessible only with difficulty, make up a considerable part of the present volume.

The alternative of "having or being" as basic orientations of our passionate strivings—of our character—had already been occupying Erich Fromm for many years before he dedicated an entire book to it at the end of his life. Prefigured by Meister Eckhart and Karl Marx (cf. E. Fromm, *On Being Human,* 1992b), he conceived of them in the 1940s as an alternative between nonproductive and productive character orientation, later as an alternative destructiveness, i.e., necrophilia, and creativity, i.e., biophilia (cf. E. Fromm, 1964a). There are statements and lectures about these alternatives as well that illustrate exactly what Fromm means by the "being mode of existence." Because they, too, are largely unknown, they were included in this volume.

Finally, this volume contains several key sections from the two books *To Have Or to Be?* and *The Art of Being,* which are of particular importance for the question of living between having and being and the question of the path to an orientation toward being; this volume also contains a previously unpublished manuscript for *To Have Or to Be?* The texts for the present volume were selected in such a way that their sequence and entirety constitute a rounded whole. Each selection and compilation of the texts pursues particular interests. One interest was to clarify life between an orientation toward having and an orientation toward being. Thus, the chapter "Essentials of a Life Between Having and Being" is a key part of the present volume. Very definite manifestations are characteristic of the orientation toward having as well as of the orientation toward being. In such cases, distinctions were made between the typical, direct manifestation of the orientation toward having and the compensatory manifestations that are characteristic of it.

• *Joy of life* is typical of the person who is oriented toward being. A person who is oriented toward having, in contrast, feels depressive and is afraid to lose his or her self, and thus tends to compensate this loss primarily through obsessive forms of consumption.

• Whoever is oriented toward being is *productively active* and lives from an inner activity, while the person who is fixated on having is determined by an odd *passivity;* in reality, he is living vicariously. In order to avoid this passivity, many people flee into busybody activity.

• *Creativity* is always a characteristic of orientation toward being; corresponding to this is the endless *boredom* of the person who is oriented toward having, a boredom that is compensated for primarily by activities in which something still happens: by "action," violence, and destructiveness.

• *Experiencing one's self* through one's own powers means the same as being oriented toward being; in contrast, the person who is oriented toward having is always fighting against a threatening *loss of self* that he attempts to ward off by narcissistic pomp.

• A *humanistic religiosity* directed against any type of reification, quantification, and idolatry of man is typical for any orientation toward being, while the person who is oriented toward having is characterized by a profound *disbelief* for which he tries to compensate with appropriated concepts of God or the gods of the Industrial Age.

• A *love of life* is the mark of all productive powers that are oriented toward being, while the person who clings to having develops panic anxieties of any separation. The fact that he will one day also be separated from life produces in the having-oriented person a characteristic *fear of death*, which usually manifests itself defensively as a denial of death, as a belief in immortality, or as a fascination with death and that which can no longer die.

In *To Have Or to Be?*, Erich Fromm discussed additional characteristics under the heading "Further Aspects of Having and Being."

The last chapter of the present collection, which deals with the "Steps toward Being," is another key point. Although important "Steps toward Being" were described in *The Art of Being,* that book gives but little attention to the fact that the steps toward being have to do with changing the bent of a person's character structure and its conscious and unconscious aspects. For this reason, the present volume also contains texts pertaining to the question of characterological change and the unconscious.

An especially relevant interest reflected in the selection and compilation of the texts of this volume is the attention drawn to "human alienation" through the market economy, which has led to the cultivation of the "marketing character." It is indeed true that the orientation toward having is characterologically related to an anal-hoarding possessiveness that seeks to acquire things only egoistically and selfishly and that does not want to give or share anything. Yet possessiveness is only one root of the orientation toward having. As Erich Fromm himself shows in part 3 of *To Have Or to Be?*, the orientation toward *having* is today far more the result of alienation caused by the marketing character. This is characterized by the fact that a person must surrender and lose more and more of his self and his individual being if he wants to be successful in the marketplace. He increasingly perceives himself as a vacuous subject that is then forced to replace his individual and subjective being with the possession of objects.

In the foreground of the orientation that results from the marketing character is the existential problematic of having to compensate for the threatening loss of one's self with the possession of objects: "If I'm not what I have, then I don't exist." On the other hand, the person who is oriented toward having and interested in possession says, "I am what I have." For both, it is true to say that they define their being by the possession of objects. Yet the various formulations point to a new dimension of existential dependency that having assumes in the marketing character. The character that is oriented toward the market place is so much more alienated from his own powers and his individual being that he uses and needs everything and anything in order to compensate for his lacking perception of self. Now, possession is not the actual motivation for the orientation toward having, but rather the necessity to use and to functionalize every relation in which a person stands—the relation to things, to other people, to intellectual, spiritual, and cultural values, to nature, to work, to God, as well as the relation to one's self—in such a way that they can constitute his being and his perception of his self, which are threatened by loss and depleted.

It is this existential dimension of orientation toward having that justifies speaking of alternative modes of *existence*. In the case of the alternative of orienting one's character toward having or being, the issue concerns psychological conditions of existence. In this case, orientation of existence toward having is marked by an existential dependency upon the objects of having and has the quality of obsessive or narcissistic dependency: If, for example, I cannot define myself as a needy person in terms of want and possession, then I am nothing and no longer have any justification for existing. The person oriented toward having is constantly threatened with the loss of his self: he stands under the threat of decompensating, of losing the ground under his feet, of falling into an abyss. By simply imagining that what one has is taken away or lost, one can test relatively easily whether one possesses what one has in the having or the being mode of existence. If the ground is thereby pulled out from under one's feet or the center of one's life is removed, then one possessed it in the having mode of existence and the loss of the beloved objects leads to a loss of one's self. To have in the being mode of existence means to have as if one did not have.

The actual problematic of the person who is oriented toward having consists in this existential dependency on the objects to which he stands in relation and that, by necessity, must form the foundation of his self and his subjective being. This is why nonmaterial values are also sought as objects of possession: the orientation toward having the right opinion, truth, concern, knowledge, correct faith, education, children, a good conscience, the grace of God, success, a good image, the need to tell others about this and that, experience, health, sickness, etc. There is nothing that could not be possessed in this mode of having. The magnanimity of the doner and the selflessness of the servant can also be at the service of the having-oriented mode of existence.

This existential dependency also explains why even worthless objects (beer-mug coasters, matchboxes, etc.) can become objects of having and being determined by nonpossession is also an expression of the orientation toward having. For example, whoever defines himself in terms of not having property in order thereby to furnish a foundation for his individual being, substitutes the nonpossession of property for his being and is characterized by the same dependence on nonpossession as the possessive person. Whoever orients himself toward nonpossession shows only that he is not capable of having a life oriented toward being. Ascetism is not a sure sign of not being capable of living in the mode of being, nor is orientation toward nonpossession the alternative to orientation toward having. The alternative of orientation toward being is and remains the capability of one's own psychological, mental, and physical productive powers to be related to the reality within and without oneself.

When possible, the texts of this volume were left in their original, unaltered form, which, in some cases, was the spoken word. All headings and divisions are the editor's. Where additions had to be made within a text, the words of the editor always appear in brackets. The abbreviated quotation citations with the text are explained in the bibliography at the end of the volume.

Special thanks are due Dr. Lance W. Garmer for his translations of this foreword and the following texts by Erich Fromm: Interview with Reif, "The Unthinkable," Interview with Assall, Interview with Ferrari, "The Problems of Surplus," Interview with Jaenecke, and Interview with Lechleitner.

Rainer Funk

On the Art of Living

*T*he idea that to live well is easy is a relatively recent one. Not that there were not always people who felt that if they achieved pleasure, power, and wealth they would be happy and that what they had to learn was not how to live well but how to be successful enough to acquire the means to the end of living well. But in contrast to those individuals and groups who practiced the principle of radical hedonism virtually all cultures had their Masters of Living and their Masters of Thinking who proclaimed that to live well was an art that had to be learned; that the learning of this art required effort, devotion, understanding, and patience; that it was the most important art to learn.

Today, in contrast, those who teach man how to live—the psychologists, sociologists, and politicians—declare that it is easy to learn. In fact there is hardly anything to learn about it beyond reading some how-to-do-it books. What has brought about this amazing change and led to the belief that it is easy to learn how to live, that the only difficult thing to learn is how to make a living?

Part of the answer lies in the practice of the machine civilization in which handwork is replaced by the servicing of machines. To make a shoe or a table was a difficult task, which one had to study for many years in order to become a master. The producers of shoes or tables who use the machine perform no difficult task; they do not have to study for years until they can function. Fewer and fewer highly skilled jobs require training that could be compared with that of a master carpenter.

The same simplicity dominates the field of consumption. Cooking, driving a car, taking pictures, almost all acts of consumption can be accomplished with little skill, effort, or concentration, provided you follow the simple rules of instruction. Why should living be an art, why should it take so much effort to learn it, when everything else is done so simply, when any child can create a whole world by pushing the button of the television set?

Yet living is *not* simple; we are endowed with a few instinctive desires whose satisfaction is necessary for the survival of the individual or the species and in this respect we do not differ from the animal. But unlike the animal we are not endowed with a built-in total instinctive equipment that tells us how to act in the general conduct of life, with a blueprint for living well. If our actions were determined by our biological necessities we would act rationally and, to mention one example, not kill each other for honor, fame, or wealth, but cooperate for the sake of survival. If our actions were determined by reason, all would be well; but our thinking is too easily the handmaid of our selfish interests and irrational passions to be a reliable guide to the art of living.

Man is a prematurely born animal and finishes his physiological birth many months after his "original" birth. Man is even less completely born mentally than physically. Psychically he needs a lifetime to give full birth to himself but he can also lose himself, stop growing at any point of his development, and end up in destructiveness, depression, lovelessness, and isolation—a crippled man.

Man is subject to the law of all life, physically and mentally, that *living is growing,* is being active; when growth stops, decay and death set in. Death in a physiological sense is easily recognized; death in a psychical sense can be recognized only by those who can sense what psychical aliveness is. The body is easily kept alive; the efforts man has to make in order to keep it alive are determined and energized by the neurophysiological structure of his brain. But he is not so impelled—or only to a much smaller degree—to keep himself growing and active psychically. He has to make a constant effort that becomes pleasurable in itself but he is not "driven" like in instinctively motivated behavior.

Considering the obstacles and difficulties that the art of living confronts us with, how could we hope to achieve it without instructions? Indeed, to teach the art of living has always been the function of Masters of Living, such as Lao-Tse, the Buddha, the Prophets, Jesus, Thomas Aquinas, Meister Eckhart, Paracelsus, Spinoza, Goethe, Marx, Schweitzer (most of these were also Masters of Thinking) who taught fundamentally the same principles, even sometimes in seemingly contradictory concepts—contradictory only to those who were interested in the words rather than in the experience to which they point.

Their principles were simple:

(1) Man's becoming fully human is the supreme and overriding goal of his life;

(2) this process of giving birth to himself leads to well-being and is accompanied by joy;

(3) only to the degree to which man overcomes hate, ignorance, greed, and selfishness and to the degree to which

his capacity for love, solidarity, reason, and courage grows, can he reach the goal;

(4) man must not only know those goals, he must practice how to attain them at every step of his life.

To be sure, one may say: Why praise these Masters of Living when the present state of the world shows how ineffectual their teaching has been? I would answer that their voices may not have been widely heard, yet had it not been for them, the human species would probably long ago have perished for lack of guidance. Much depends, for the solution of our dilemma, on our beginning again to learn from them, not because they "represent the tradition" but because they represent the accumulated insight, wisdom, and knowledge of the human race. Their position, if taken seriously, is revolutionary and radical, without which purely political radicalism must remain ineffective; however, their teachings will become even more ineffectual if they are not related to radical changes in our economic, social and political structure which has become an ever-growing obstacle to personal growth and well-being.

I am not appealing for submitting to religious and philosophical authorities of the past, but to learn from them. This is an appeal to think critically, to wake up and see that we are actually determined by life-hostile "masters" who masquerade as Masters of Living—those who have become famous and powerful by their failure to become fully human.

There is one more reason why it is believed that it is easy to learn the art of living. This reason, in contrast to the previous one, is deeply unconscious. It lies in the belief that man is not important, or to put it differently, that living is not important. This belief must necessarily be unconscious because it contradicts the prevailing and generally accepted ideology of the importance of human life. It is not generally noticed that this ideology covers the fact that man has become an adjunct to the machine, a part of it which cannot (yet) be replaced by a mechanical part, and that he does not rule the machine, but it and the whole economic system rule him. That he is important as a cog that is necessary for the functioning of the whole but not as an alive, rich, productive human being; that he has become a commodity whose value lies in his saleability. He is to function well and has to be alive and satisfied to the degree and in the kind that is necessary for his functioning. Indeed when "functioning well" has replaced "being well," why should it be worth making an effort to learn "the art of living?"

Unpublished paper.

Human Alienation

Market Economy and Its Effects on People

The most important fact for understanding both the character and the secret religion of contemporary human society is the change in the social character from the earlier era of capitalism to the second part of the twentieth century. The authoritarian-obsessive-hoarding character that had begun to develop in the sixteenth century, and continued to be the dominant character structure at least in the middle classes until the end of the nineteenth century, was slowly blended with or replaced by the *marketing character*. I have called this phenomenon the "marketing character" because it is based on experiencing oneself as a commodity, and one's value not as "use value" but as "exchange value."

To Have Or to Be?, p. 147.

Our modern economy is not governed by a market where people sit and sell their wares, but what you might call a "National Commodity Market," in which prices and production are determined by demand. This national market is the regulating factor for modern economy. The prices are not determined by any economic group who says that and that must be paid. This is something exceptional in wartime or in certain situations. The price or "while existence" is determined by the operation of the market, which constantly tends to equalize and to balance itself up to a certain point.

What is the meaning of all this in psychological terms? What happens on the market is that all things appear as commodities. What is the difference between a thing and a commodity? This glass of water here is a thing that at the moment I can use to hold water and so on. It is very useful to me. It is not particularly pretty, but it is what it is. However, as a commodity it is something I can buy, which has a certain price, and I perceive of it not only as this thing, as something that has a certain *use value* as they say, but as a commodity that has a certain *exchange value*. It appears as a commodity in the market, and its function as a commodity is in the sense that I can describe it as a fifty-cent or twenty-five-cent thing. That is, so to say, I can express this thing in terms of money, or in terms of an abstraction. In fact, if you take your own attitude toward things and if you analyze it a little, you will find that you relate yourself to things to a large extent, not as concrete things, but as commodities. You perceive already of a thing in terms of its abstract money value, in terms of its exchange value.

The Pathology of Normalcy, pp. 61–62.

Also the living being becomes a commodity on the "personality market." The principle of evaluation is the same on both the personality and the commodity markets: on the one, personalities are offered for sale; on the other, commodities. Value in both cases is their exchange value, for which "use value" is a necessary but not a sufficient condition.

Although the proportion of skill and human qualities on the one hand and personality on the other hand as prerequisites for success varies, the "personality factor" always plays a decisive role. Success depends largely on how well persons sell themselves on the market, how well they get their personalities across, how nice a "package" they are; whether they are cheerful, "sound," "aggressive," "reliable," or "ambitious"; furthermore, what their family backgrounds are, what clubs they belong to, and whether they know the "right" people.

The type of personality required depends to some degree on the special field in which a person may choose to work. A stockbroker, a salesperson, a secretary, a railroad executive, a college professor, or a hotel manager must each offer a different kind of personality that, regardless of their differences, must fulfill one condition: to be in demand.

What shapes one's attitude toward oneself is the fact that skill and equipment for performing a given task are not sufficient; one must be able to "put one's personality across" in competition with many others in order to have success. If it were enough for the purpose of making a living to rely on what one knows and what one can do, one's self-esteem would be in proportion to one's capacities, that is, to one's use value. But since success depends largely on how one sells one's personality, one experiences oneself as a commodity or, rather, simultaneously as the seller *and* the commodity to be sold. A person is not concerned with his or her life and happiness, but with becoming salable.

The aim of the marketing character is complete adaptation, so as to be desirable under all conditions of the personality market. The marketing character personalities do not even *have* egos (as people in the nineteenth century did) to hold onto, that belong to them, that do not change. For they constantly change their egos, according to the principle: "I am as you desire me."

Those with the marketing character structure are without goals, except moving, doing things with the greatest efficiency; if asked *why* they must move so fast, why things have to be done with the greatest efficiency, they have no genuine answer, but offer rationalizations, such as, "in order to create more jobs," or "in order to keep the company growing." They have little interest (at least consciously) in philosophical or religious questions, such as *why* one lives, and *why* one is going in this direction rather than in another. They have their big, ever-changing egos, but none has a self, a core, a sense of identity. The "identity crisis" of modern society is actually the crisis produced by the fact that its members have become selfless instruments, whose identity rests upon their participation in the corporations (or other giant bureaucracies), as a primitive individual's identity rested upon membership in the clan.

To Have Or to Be?, pp. 147–48.

The average person today feels alone. He feels himself to be a commodity, by which I mean he feels that his value depends on his success, depends on his salability, depends on approval by others. He feels that it does not depend on the intrinsic or what you might call *use* value of his personality, not on his powers, not on his capacity to love, not on his human qualities—except if he can sell them, except if he can be successful, except if he is approved by others.

This accounts for the fact that the self-esteem of most people today is very shaky. They do not feel themselves worthy because of their own conviction: "This is me, this is my capacity to love, this is my capacity to think and to feel," but because they are approved by others, because they can sell themselves, because others say: "This is a wonderful man" or "a wonderful woman."

Naturally, when the feeling of self-esteem is dependent upon others it becomes uncertain. Each day is a new battle because each day you have to convince someone, and you have to prove to yourself, that you are all right. To use an analogy, I would suggest that you consider how handbags would feel on a counter in a store. The handbag of one particular style, of which may have been sold, would feel elated in the evening; and the other handbag, of a style a little out of fashion or a little too expensive or which, for some reason or other, had not been sold, would be depressed. The one handbag would feel: "I am wonderful," and the other handbag would feel: "I am unworthy," and yet the "wonderful" handbag may not be more beautiful or more useful or have any better intrinsic quality than the other one. The unsold handbag would feel it was not wanted. In our analogy, a handbag's sense of value would depend on its success, on how may purchasers, for one reason or another, preferred the one to the other.

In human terms that means that one must be peculiar, that one's own personality must always be open to change in order to conform to the latest model. That is why parents often feel embarrassed when they are with their children. The children know the latest models better than the parents do. But the parents are very ready to be taught, to be told, to learn. They, like the children, listen to the latest quotations on the personality market. And where do you find these market quotations? Where do you read them? In the movies, in the liquor ads, in the clothing ads, in the indications of the ways that important people dress and talk.

Man and Woman, pp. 11–12.

Everything has become an operation, everything has to have a function and a use. There is no sense of identity, but rather just a spiritual void. People have neither convictions nor genuine goals. The marketing character is the perfectly alienated human being. He is concerned only with manipulating and functioning. That is exactly the type that meets social needs. One can say that most people turn out to be as society wishes them so that they can be successful. Society fabricates types of people just as it fabricates styles of shoes or of clothes or of automobiles, that is, as goods that are in demand. A person learns already as a child what type is in demand.   Interview with Reif, pp. 27–28.

The term "marketing character" is by no means the only one to describe this type. It can also be described by using a Marxian term, the *alienated character;* persons of this character are alienated from their work, from themselves, from other human beings, and from nature. In psychiatric terms the marketing person could be called a schizoid character; but the term may be slightly misleading, because a schizoid person living with other schizoid persons and performing well and being successful, because of his schizoid character, entirely lacks the feeling of uneasiness that the schizoid character has in a more "normal" environment.

To Have Or to Be?, p. 151.

Reason and Intelligence

The marketing character goal, *"proper functioning"* under the given circumstances, makes them respond to the world mainly cerebrally. Reason in the sense of *understanding* is an exclusive quality of *homo sapiens; manipulative intelligence* as a tool for the achievement of practical purposes is common to animals and humans. Manipulative intelligence without reason is dangerous because it makes people move in directions that may be self-destructive from the standpoint of reason. In fact, the more brilliant the uncontrolled manipulative intelligence is, the more dangerous it is.

To Have Or to Be?, pp. 149–50.

Reasons discern causes and relationships, how they are and why they are that way. Manipulative intelligence is concerned only with how a person can better use things for himself. Reason is specifically human and is effective only insofar as man has freed himself from irrational passions and desires. Insofar as man is avaricious, his reason cannot have an effect.

His manipulative intelligence, on the other hand, is excited and increased by greediness. The greedy person is sly; the reasonable person is smart; the dependent person becomes stupid, the independent person becomes wiser. Ultimately, the distinction between reason and manipulative intelligence issues from a moral problem. The more man wants to *have* and the more he makes himself dependent on things and is bound to them, the more he will become a prisoner of things. Stupidity is not a result of deficient innate intelligence, but rather of deficient freedom. Reason develops only in freedom, not only in freedom from external coercive forces, but also from internal coercive forces of confinement in its numerous manifestations. This distinction is easily forgotten in industrial society, where manipulative intelligence is the ruling type of thinking. If we take this distinction seriously, then one would be confronted with the unpleasant realization that we still usually employ our thinking like animals (this is especially clear in the case of the primates), and only a small minority has attained a human level of thinking. Intelligence makes us only the cleverest animal, symbolized in the Biblical myth as a serpent that "was cleverer than all other animals." Manipulative intelligence can be useful, it can lead to an improvement of life, but it can also be the path to hell; cognizant reason is a child of freedom, and its development leads to ever-growing freedom.

Interview with Reif, pp. 43–43a.

The Split between Affect and Intellect

Why we have developed in a top-heavy way is a very interesting question. Why, within three or four centuries, has all our emphasis shifted more and more to intellect and more and more away from rationality and intensity of affect?

There is not space to discuss this, but it has a great deal to do with our mode of production, with our increasing emphasis on technique, with our necessity to develop intellect for purposes of science and science for the purposes of technique. We cannot quite separate the society, in which production becomes the paramount purpose, from human development in which intellect becomes the paramount value. But if we are to overcome our moral problem today, we must make a very serious effort to overcome the split between affect and intellect. We must restore the person to his totality or, as I would rather say, to his reality. I am not a mind and a body. I am I, and you are you, and my heart and my feelings can be just as rational as my thought, and my thought can be just as irrational as my heart. But, I cannot even speak of my heart and my thought because they are one, they are only two aspects of the same phenomenon. There is one logic, one rationality, and one irrationality that pervades them both. Whether we study psychosomatic illness or whether we study the phenomena of mass hysteria, it is all the same. Thought is made stupid by feeling and thought can be enlightened by feeling and vice versa. First, I think we must be aware of this problem because most of us are not. Most of us are somewhat embarrassed about having feelings at all.

Sometimes one can see in psychoanalysis that a person consciously, on the surface, thinks he is very happy. He loves his wife, he loves his children and he is very happy.

If you dig a little deeper, this follows: He makes a good living, he is successful and is respected; therefore, he assumes that he has to feel happy. So his feeling happy is actually an assumption about feeling happy. Then you go a step deeper and you might say to this man: "Look here, I have watched your face now for several sessions and I think you look awfully sad and depressed. What are you sad about?" Then you might find that this person who has said that for twenty years he has never cried, suddenly remembers something from his childhood, something that was always alive in him, and cries uncontrollably. You find that to protect himself from sadness he had to protect himself from feeling, and over this protection from feeling he put an illusion of feeling, something that was nothing but a logical assumption.

The Moral Responsibility of Modern Man, pp. 11–12.

There are also false feelings. As an example, I will describe a very simple hypnotic experiment. Mr. A is being hypnotized. Let us assume that it is nine o'clock in the morning. He is told by the hypnotist that this afternoon, at three o'clock, he will take off his coat and, unless some other suggestions are given, he will forget that this happened. Now let us assume that you meet Mr. A, who has been hypnotized in the morning at nine o'clock, at half past two. You talk with him about the weather, whatever you are interested in at the moment. At just a minute before three o'clock, Mr. A will say: "Isn't it an awfully hot day? Really, I have to take off my coat." Now, if it is really a warm day you will think this is very sensible, or if it is a very cold day but the heating is so hot that you can't stand it, you will still think that his reaction is very sensible. However, if it's a day that is not too hot and your building is not overheated, you will be very surprised that Mr. A feels it is so hot and you might think that he is running a fever and suggest that he go to the doctor. Nonetheless, you are convinced that Mr. A feels hot and has a need to take off his coat. If, however, you had been present at nine o'clock during the hypnotic session, you would know that this whole feeling of being hot was only induced by the suggestion of the hypnotist. Still, there is this interesting phenomenon that Mr. A has the need to make what he does appear rational. Mr. A cannot simply, spontaneously take off his coat. No, he has to find a reason for it. If you were not present in the morning you would be convinced that he really feels warm.

This is only a special case of what happens, many times, even without hypnosis. We believe we feel something which we really do not feel—simply because we follow suggestions, public opinion, and the like. Then we have to find a reason for these actions that seem to be motivated by the feeling we rationalize. For example, if you belong to the highbrows, then you probably feel that Picasso is very beautiful and great art. Well, for all I know it may be so. However, if you are indoctrinated that this is something beautiful, then you look at the paintings and you feel that they are wonderful, but you *feel nothing* really. All that happens is that you have a *thought* of feeling something and most people are not quite able to differentiate or distinguish between a genuine feeling—which is a reality, which corresponds to something that goes on in the whole physiological system of the person—and the thought of a feeling, which is almost like a real feeling, except that it isn't.

Now, if you try to observe in the only laboratory we all have within us, that is, our own life, you will find that many times one has a conviction that he feels something— interest, love, joy, this, that and the other, when actually he has only thoughts about feelings. There are many occasions when your feelings were pseudofeelings; you felt as you were supposed to feel by indoctrination of the culture, and there are many situations where you feel what you are supposed to feel and don't know the difference between authentic feelings and pseudofeelings.

"Problems of Aging," p. 12.

I mean by intellectuals people who talk about things that they don't feel, people who are mainly cerebrally related to the world and to other people, mainly manipulating thought rather than experiencing the creative fusion of thought and feeling; I could say, to use an image, that the heart and the brain of intellectuals are not connected, or, in philosophical terms, they are alienated. What they think are mainly thoughts that are not related to feelings; actually, in a way, it is one definition of schizophrenia.

I believe, indeed, that our society offers the picture of a low-grade chronic schizophrenia. While society in the nineteenth century offered the picture of a low-grade general hysteria, which is expressed in styles—for instance in expressing bodily all sorts of feelings from the fainting of women to the orators of the stage—today the style is, you might say, schizoid, with no emotions shown and often not felt, and certain separation between affective life and thought, which can lead to some of the most terrible phenomena of the modern world, namely that people are capable of thinking coldly of the destruction of the whole world. That is the great change in style between the nineteenth century and the twentieth century, which I am sure has to do with the different socioeconomic structure.

The fact is that most people today are employees, high or low, who do what they are told or what the rules tell them and feel as little as possible since feelings disturb the smooth functioning of the machine. In industrial societies, for which it is essential that the machine functions smoothly, since every unsmoothness, every friction in the machine, costs money, people must train themselves to have as few emotions as possible because an emotion costs money.   "Interview with Khoury," pp. 37–38.

Instead of being related, being in touch with love, with hate, with fear, with doubt, with all of the basic experiences of man, we all are rather detached. We are related to an abstraction, that is to say we are not related at all. We live in a vacuum and fill the vacuum, fill the gap with words, with abstract signs of values, with routine, which helps us out from the embarrassment.

In this situation there is one other thing we do: we are sentimental. *Sentimentality is feeling under the condition of complete detachment.* Unless you are really insane, you have feeling, but if you are as detached, as remote, as unrelated to things as I was just talking about, then you have a very peculiar situation. You have feelings, but you do not refer really, concretely to something that is the reality. You are sentimental. Your feelings overflow. They appear somewhere. We use catch words, "honesty," "patriotism," or on the other hand words like "revolution," or any number of words that are abstract concepts, which at the moment have no concrete meaning. They are stimulation words, which make you weep, which make you howl, which make you do anything, and yet it is a performance in which the feeling is not really related to something with which you are concerned, but which is an empty thing.

It is like a person crying at the movies when the heroine loses a chance to make 100,000 dollars and people cry and the same people in real life can witness a great tragedy around themselves and around their own lives, and they do not cry, and do not feel anything, because they are really unrelated. They are not concerned. They live in that vacuum of abstraction, of alienation from the reality of feelings. Yet they have feelings, so there are some catchwords, some stimuli, some situations provoking this feeling, but not in the sense that I cry because I am really related to unhappiness, but am quite detached. I live in a vacuum, but the feeling that is in me needs some outlet, and so I cry where there is some occasion without really being related to anything. I think that is the essence of sentimentality that can be observed so frequently in modern culture, when you see people who give the impression of being rather detached, rather remote, of not being related to anything particularly, and then you find these outbursts of feeling.

The Pathology of Normalcy, pp. 73–74.

Love as a Commodity

What happens to *love* in this situation of self-alienation, of unrelatedness? I think what we see is that love is, so to speak, divided into two channels; one, it becomes identified with sex, and you get the many books in which you learn sexual techniques in order to enhance love in marriage; or love becomes a rather sexless unerotic thing in which two people get along well with each other, and if they happen to be a woman and a man, they get married, and call that love. It is nice companionship at best, but there is not much of any spark, of any particular glowing element, which in older times was connected with the idea of love.

The Pathology of Normalcy, pp. 86–87.

Love expresses hundred, thousands of different things. Now I am not at all saying that a feeling cannot be summed up in a word, but that each person's love for another person is a different love; that goes without saying. Yet the problem is that we have only *one* word for this entire area of feeling called "love," which extends from affection to the deepest active relationship that, on the other hand, is sometimes considered as a secondary product of a sexual relationship.

Today, people have largely forgotten the illusion that sexuality as such has something to do with love, and—especially among men—it certainly has more to do with narcissism than with love. But there is no differentiation whatsoever within this concept for us today. At least there is quite an elementary differentiation in other languages, namely, the differentiation between maternal and erotic love. We do not differentiate. A mother loves her child just as she loves a lover or sometimes loves her husband. We always use one and the same word.

In Greek, there is the distinction between *eros* and *agape;* in Hebrew, there is the distinction between *ahabah* (which comes from the root for to glow) and *rachamim* (which comes from the root *rechem,* the womb). There is a clear differentiation here between erotic and maternal love. At least that is something, and, in any case, it is better than the poverty of our one word "love" for everything that exists in human relationships.

"Love" is also an indirect expression for what people say—to use another indirect expression—in English "to sleep with someone." This is rather incorrect: to sleep is exactly what one doesn't want to do. Sleeping may perhaps be a by-product, but it is not the goal of the activity. Non-obscene expressions are indirect, but the direct ones are obscene. Whoever wants to tell another person directly about a sexual relationship must say something obscene, and whoever does not want to express himself obscenely must paradoxically use an analogy (and often even an incorrect one). This shows that sexuality is degraded among us.

"The Unthinkable," pp. 20–22.

Since the marketing characters have no deep attachment to themselves or to others, they do not care, in any deep sense of the word, not because they are so selfish but because their relations to others and to themselves are so thin. This may also explain why they are not concerned with the dangers of nuclear and ecological catastrophes, even though they know all the data that point to these dangers. That they are not concerned with the danger to their personal lives might still be explained by the assumption that they have great courage and unselfishness; but the lack of concern even for their children and grandchildren excludes such explanation. The lack of concern of all these levels is the result of the loss of any emotional ties, even to those "nearest" to them. The fact is, nobody is close to the marketing characters; neither are they close to themselves.

The puzzling question why contemporary human beings love to buy and to consume, and yet are so little attached to what they buy, finds its most significant answer in the marketing character phenomenon. The marketing characters' lack of attachment also makes them indifferent to things. What matters is perhaps the prestige or the comfort that things give, but things per se have no substance. They are utterly expendable, along with friends or lovers, who are expendable, too, since no deeper tie exists to any of them.   *To Have Or to Be?*, p. 149.

How does this "marketing orientation" affect the relationship between the sexes, between men and women? I think, in the first place, that a great deal of what goes under the name of love is a seeking for success, for approval. One needs someone to tell one not only at four o'clock in the afternoon but also at eight and at ten and at twelve: "You're fine, you're all right, you are doing well." That is one factor. The other factor is that one also proves one's value by choosing the right person. One needs to be the latest model oneself, but one then has a right also and a duty to fall in love with the latest model. That can be put as crudely as it was put by a boy of eighteen who was asked what the ambition of his life was. He said be wanted to buy a better car; he wanted to change from a Ford to a Buick so that he could pick up a better class of girls. Well, this boy was at least frank, but I think he expressed something that, in a more subtle way, determines the choice of partners to a large extent in our culture.

The marketing orientation has another effect on the relationship between the sexes. In the marketing orientation everything is patterned, and we are eager to live up to the latest model and to act in the latest way. Accordingly the roles we choose, particularly our sex roles, are highly patterned, but the patterns are not even or uniform. Frequently they are conflicting. Man ought to be aggressive in business and tender at home. He ought to live for his work but not be tired in the evening when he comes home. He ought to be ruthless with his customers and competitors, but he ought to be very honest with his wife and children. He ought to be liked by everyone, and yet he should have the deepest feeling for his family. The poor man tries to live up to these patterns. Only the fact that he does not take them too seriously probably protects him from going crazy. The same holds true for women. They too have to live patterns that are as contradictory as those for the males.

There always were, of course, in every culture, patterns for what was considered to be male and female, masculine and feminine; but formerly these patterns had at least a certain stability. In a culture in which we depend so much on the *latest* pattern, on being just right, on approval, on fitting in with what is expected, the real qualities that belong to our male or female roles become obscured. Very little specific is left in the relationship between men and women.

If the choices in relationships between men and women are made on the basis of market orientation, of highly patterned roles, one thing must happen: people get bored. Many people see only two solutions for this boredom. They avoid being bored by using any of the many avenues of escape our culture offers. They go to parties, make contacts, drink, play cards, listen to the radio, and so kid themselves every day, every evening. Or—and this is partly a matter of what social class they belong to—they think things are improved by a change of partner. The think this or that marriage was no good because they got the wrong partner, and they suppose that a change of partner will dispel boredom. People do not see that the main question is not: "Am I loved?" which is to a large extent the question: "Am I approved of? Am I protected? Am I admired?" The main question is: "Can I love?"

That is indeed difficult. To be loved and to "fall in love" is very simple for a while until you get boring and bored. But to love, "to stand in love," as it were, is indeed difficult, although not superhuman; in fact, it is the most essential human quality. If one cannot be alone with oneself, if one cannot be genuinely interested in others and in oneself, then one cannot be together with anyone else without being bored after a certain time. If the relationship between the sexes becomes a refuge for the loneliness and isolation of the individual, it has very little to do with the potentialities that the real relationship between male and female implies.

"Man and Woman," pp. 13–15.

In German, "love" has the same root as "praise," but also as "joy" and "freedom." These words express an experience, a complex of experiences. There is no love in which there is no joy, freedom, and praise. There is an old French folk song that says "L'amour est l'enfant de la liberté" (Love is the child of freedom). Love and freedom are brought together in this folk song. Today, this inner, most profound connection between love and freedom is hardly experienced in this way. Quite the contrary. Most people are afraid that they will lose their freedom when they love, and they cannot believe that love at the same time indicates the greatest development of freedom.   "The Unthinkable," p. 24.

Origins of the
Having Mode of Existence

Patriarchal Society

*E*ssential to the desire to have is that one first wants to have more and more, thereby necessarily coming into conflict with the interests of everyone else on an individual level within a society as well as on an international level between nations. By their nature, greed and the desire to have are characterized by their limitlessness. Physiological needs are limited by nature. We might be a little hungry or tremendously hungry, but at some point we are full. This is also true of sexuality; this is also true for all physical needs.

But our industrial complex has invented a system in order to maintain itself and to have the requisite profits, and constantly creates new needs. If I have an automobile, I want to have two; when I have a small automobile, I want a big one; and after I have that, then I want a yacht and later I even want an airplane.   Interview with Assall.

Our judgments are extremely biased because we live in a society that rests on private property, profit, and power as the pillars of its existence. To acquire, to own, and to make a profit are the sacred and inalienable rights of the individual in the industrial society. What the sources of property are does not matter; nor does possession impose any obligations on the property owners. While private ownership is supposed to be a natural and universal category, it is in fact an exception rather than the rule if we consider the whole of human history (including prehistory), and particularly the cultures outside Europe in which economy was not life's main concern.   *To Have Or to Be?*, p. 69.

Societies that were not oriented toward having are primarily the prehistoric ones, i.e., hunters, gatherers, and sedentary farmers, which constituted the only social formation until the founding of cities, that is to say, until patriarchal predominance, the exploitation of man by man, and the control over them. Indeed, there are quite comprehensive studies today about historical periods in which women were not yet oppressed and where a matriarchal or *matricentric* order probably existed in a series of societies. Not even the idea of exploitation existed in these societies, for the simple reason that it was pointless. Whom was one supposed to exploit? In an economic system in which man and woman work on equal terms, it would be senseless to have others work for one: one would thereby condemn oneself to laziness. Quite contrary to general opinion, though, man is not lazy by nature; rather, he has a deep need to work, to do something, to create.

Exploitation, class differences—and thus envy—did not arise until there was considerable surplus—at about the fourth or fifth century B.C.—and today rule throughout the entire world, albeit with a few exceptions. Patriarchy is actually the prototype of all exploitation, not only of a class, but of one-half of humanity by another. I believe that one can confidently say that exploitation in general will not be stopped until patriarchy is stopped—which is by no means yet the case today—since patriarchy itself *is* that human behavior by which a person uses another for his own purposes.   Interview with Reif 1977, pp. 1–2.

Biologically speaking, man is a failure because a woman is capable of creating and man lacks that, that capacity for creating something; the man is, as far as his experience goes, sterile, because it is purely theoretical knowledge that for the production of a child his semen is necessary. The child is practically entirely the creature of the mother, who gives life to the child; the father does not give life to the child. Most men repress their awareness of this wish because they want to keep up the illusion of their superiority! You felt it consciously, but most men repress completely the fact that they are biologically inferior. They need to silence their own biological inferiority feeling by power, by dominating and exploiting the women, to prove again and again, every day, that they are not inferior.

                     Interview with Khoury, p. 45.

Women were more helpless than men, due to the fact that they had to bear and care for children. Women were also extraordinarily more limited than men in their freedom to begin something different, to take up new types of work. Men used this fact very much to their advantage and then began to enslave women at the moment when there was generally a greater surplus and when it became possible to have another person work for one.

   In agrarian society—ca. 9000 to 7000 B.C.E.—exploitation did not yet exist, because everyone had to work in order to live. Exploitation first began when the surplus was so large that men could begin to establish a state, to have slaves, to form governments, to wage war, and to take prisoners. Women were also among the prisoners, despite the paradoxical situation that men say they need women. This is rather similar to a gentleman's saying to his butler that he needs him, although he feels far superior to him.

Of course, men also invented an ideology, as do all victorious groups. They declared that their victory was entirely logical, entirely natural, since women were just weaker, more vain, more irrational, more dependent, and whatever other descriptions that came from the mouths of men during the age of patriarchy. Freud provided the height of the rationalization of masculine war propaganda when he saw the superiority of the man in anatomy. Since one cannot change anatomy, because it is given, if not by God, then certainly by nature, there was no other choice than to attest to woman her inferiority and subsequently comfort her with the fact that, in one form or another, she finds in man that which she alone does not have. Many women also allowed themselves to become convinced of this, although it is rather absurd.   "The Unthinkable," pp. 5–9.

Remnants of matriarchal structure can also be shown to exist in contemporary social-patriarchal life. One example is the Jews, who continue to consider their ancestry according to matriarchal law: whoever is a Jew is Jewish by virtue of his mother, not of his father. That is a remnant of a matrilocal view of things. There are also still many maternal elements in the Catholic Church that Protestantism then excised. In Catholicism, people speak of the "Mother Church." The Pope sits, so to speak, on two stools. On the one hand, he is the loving mother who forgives everyone; on the other hand, though, he is also an authoritarian patriarchal figure who passes judgment.

Sufficiently many examples can be found that show there were long periods in human history when women were not exploited, when nobody at all was exploited, and when women were on completely equal terms or even ruled. Yet, despite the tremendous abundance of material in literature and archaeology that proves this fact, male scholars have been completely unobjective and—at least to a large degree—still are. Interview with Reif 1977, pp. 3–4.

Whether a matriarchal or patriarchal system is better is hard to say. In fact, I think the question in this form is wrong because you might say that the matriarchal system emphasizes the elements of natural ties, of natural equality, of love; and the patriarchal system then emphasizes the elements of civilization, of thought, of the state, of invention and industries and, in many ways, of progress, in comparison with the old matriarchal culture.

The aim of mankind must be not to have any kind of hierarchy, either matriarchal or patriarchal. We must come to a situation in which the sexes relate to each other without any attempt to dominate. Only in that way can they develop their real differences, their real polarity.

Indeed, I believe that the only answer to the problem, speaking in somewhat general terms is to work toward a concept of polarity in the relationship between the two sexes. You would not say of the positive or negative pole of an electric current that one is inferior to the other. You would say that the field between them is caused by their polarity, and that this very polarity is the basis of productive forces. In the same sense the two sexes and that for which they stand (the male and the female aspect in the world, in the universe, and in each of us) are two poles that have to retain their difference, their polarity, in order to exercise the fruitful dynamism, the productive force, that springs from that very polarity.

"Man and Woman," p. 21 and 10.

Private Property

In neolithic society around 8000 B.C.E., the idea of private property was still inconceivable. The concept of ownership of private property—the concept that someone has something that belongs only to him and that is therefore private, i.e., that what he owns can be taken away by someone else—did not exist in neolithic society. Nor does it exist in many societies that still exist, such as in the case of the North American Pueblo Indians. The concept can be neither conceived nor, of course, expressed, because the institution of private property only arises with a certain level of social development.

Of course, this is even far more so the case for a word like "capital." "Capital" is quite a modern concept, even though the thing to which it refers also existed to a certain degree in Roman antiquity. It refers to assets and goods that can be used to produce other goods at a profit for the producer. It is thus quite a new word, because it belongs to quite a recent form of social life. In early and prehistory, the concept of having did not yet at all exist in the sense that I have something that belongs to me, something that I am proud to own, something that I can do with as I please, something that I can even destroy, which, although economically senseless, is nevertheless a reality.

"The Unthinkable," pp. 2–3.

As long as the standard of living is minimal, the average person has no property other than his wife and children. That is all that he owns. But when the standard of living rises, then his wife and children are no longer the only objects of his possession. The penumbra of possession extends to friends, sociability, travel, art objects, to God, and his own ego. This means that many more objects of possession exist than under primitive conditions. A peasant in India usually owns only his wife and children, and he produces more and more children because they are his only capital, the only thing that he can produce without having to spend a great deal.   Interview with Reif 1977, p. 23.

The nature of the having mode of existence follows from the nature of private property. In this mode of existence all that matters is my acquisition of property and my unlimited right to keep what I have acquired. The having mode excludes others; it does not require any further effort on my part to keep my property or to make productive use of it. The Buddha has described this mode of behavior as craving, the Jewish and Christian religions as coveting; it transforms everybody and everything into something dead and subject to another's power.   *To Have Or to Be?*, pp. 76–77.

That which one *has* is one's *property*, and inasmuch as everybody "has" his body it could be argued that property is rooted in the very physical existence of man. But even though this would appear to be a good argument for the universality of property, it hardly serves this purpose, because it is not correct: A slave does not own his body; it can be used, sold, destroyed, according to his owner's will and whim. The slave, in this respect, differs from even the most exploited worker; the latter does not own his body energy because he is forced to sell it to the owner of capital who buys his working power. (However, since he has no choice, under the conditions of capitalism, one must admit that even his ownership of his body is questionable.) What does it mean that I own something when somebody else owns the right to use what I have?

A clear understanding of property has been greatly obscured by the passionate feelings related to the revolutionary demands for abolition of private property. Many people have thought that their personal property—their clothes, books, furniture, and so on, even their spouses—would be taken away and "nationalized." Marx and other socialists had never proposed anything as silly as that the personal property or things one uses should be socialized; they were referring to the ownership of capital—i.e., the means of production that enable an owner to produce commodities that were socially undesirable and to impose on the worker his conditions because he, the owner, "gave" him work.

The Art of Being, pp. 96–97.

In the so-called socialist countries, private property has not at all been abolished. It does not matter for the worker whether the factories have been taken over by the state or belong to a large company. In a factory that has been taken over by the state, the worker has just as little to say as in a western factory, even less. Furthermore, state socialism's big appeal is directed toward the instinct to possess. Having a car is much more the anticipation of a Russian than of an American. The Russians are awaiting the happiness of an era when everyone owns a car.

No new society is created by the abolition of so-called private property as such—the sense of property remains. The real question is whether the emphasis is changed from having to being, as can be encountered in many primitive societies or even to a certain degree in medieval society. It depends on one's attitude toward life, on joy of being, on genuine activity. And this depends to a crucial extent on the structure of a society.

The pat formula of the abolition of private property or of the socialization of the means of production has essentially proven to be a fiction. As we have already said, it is basically the same whether a factory belongs to an owner or to the

state. All that matters is whether, and to what extent, a person's *inner* attitude shifts from having to being. When having is no longer important, then it does not matter whether one person has a little more than another. On the contrary: precisely the people who say that everyone must have exactly the same amount are very often just covert proxies of a possessive attitude. Envy motivates them. They are so obsessed with the importance of having that they can conceive of justice only under the condition that nobody has a little more than anybody else. These are basically envious people who live altogether in an orientation toward having but who rationalize their envy as "justice."
Interview with Reif 1977, pp. 30–32.

Having Mode and Language

In many cultures and languages, such as in Hebrew, the word "have" does not even exist. Even today, one says in Hebrew, "it is to me," rather than "I have." In very many languages, the word for "have" developed only in the course of evolution; it was never a part of the language from the beginning. This means that the word "have" can always be shown to have its origin later in the history of language, never earlier. It would be very interesting to investigate whether this change in language has to do with the fact that the word "have" does not appear until the advent of private ownership and that the word "have" does not exist in societies in which private ownership does not yet exist.

Indeed, language is the crystallization of man's feelings and moods. Wherever people do not have the feeling of having, language does not contain the word "have," but rather other forms that express this more functionally. Of course, everyone in every society must have something. I must have clothes, as primitive as they may be, or jewelry, which is not of the least importance, but is something of the highest importance—the need for jewelry is quite an elementary need of man. Songs, melodies, and ballads are always a part of social property, but they are property in the sense that they are regarded not as possessions, but rather as functional property. This song is *by me*, but I do not keep it for myself.

Now, the more the orientation toward having grows in society, the more the meaning of the word "have" must also grow. This development continues so that, in the end, much more is expressed in our modern languages by "have" and only very little with "be."

Interview with Reif 1977, p. 18.

A certain change in the emphasis of having and being is apparent in the growing use of nouns and the decreasing use of verbs in western languages in the past few centuries. A noun is the proper denotation for a thing. I can say that I *have* things: for instance that I have a table, a house, a book, a car. The proper denotation for an activity, a process, is a verb: for instance I am, I love, I desire, I hate, etc. Yet ever more frequently an *activity* is expressed in terms of *having;* that is, a noun is used instead of a verb. But to express an activity by *to have* in connection with a noun is an erroneous use of language, because processes and activities cannot be possessed; they can only be experienced.

To Have Or to Be?, p. 20.

Before the seventeenth century, the word "success" existed only in the sense of "to follow," or "to succeed," "something happens if I do something." If I continue to push the object on the table, then it follows that it will fall off. But that has nothing to do with the concept that is today the most important one, i.e., that a person has "success." Such a thing could not yet be said in the sixteenth century, because the entire idea of success, or of distinguishing oneself and of being superior to other people, was not at all possible in the language of the Middle Ages (which still bore the stamp of religion). The entirely new concept did not come into being until the beginning of competition and the start of the rise of the middle class. A man is successful. Today, we have the feeling that "success" must be one of the oldest words in the history of mankind. If two women in a primitive society have molded and beautifully decorated a vase, then we would say that the woman who decorated it more beautifully is the most successful woman. But such a notion is unthinkable in any "primitive" society.

To give another example: there is a horse race among the American Pueblo Indians. But when two horses cross the finish line at about the same time, then they are both winners. The Pueblos are not interested in whether one is better than the other; and, indeed, this is also much more realistic, since there is no difference if one or the other is ahead by a millimeter. Practically speaking, both ran equally quickly. Of course, this is only possible if the concept of success does not exist, since, from the standpoint of success, the person who was ahead by one millimeter has won and was successful.

By this, I want to say that concepts such as "success," which appear to us to be natural in our language, are purely sociologically conditioned concepts that exist just as infrequently in many other societies as the concept of "exploitation." They have grown out of the activity of a society and will also vanish in another society and activity. Every society has the greatest skill for the words that are particularly important for its social structure.

"The Unthinkable," pp. 18–20.

To Have Or to Be?

Having versus Being

*I*t is necessary to distinguish between existential and historical dichotomies. Existential dichotomies, for example, refer to the ideal of the complete development of all people. It is an existential that man is endowed with many more possibilities that he can realize during his lifetime. A person would have to have three, four, indeed a thousand lives in order to be able to develop himself entirely. In a word: there is a series that can be explained by the human condition.

From these, one must distinguish those that are historically conditioned and ultimately founded on the basic that has so far dominated history—with the exception of prehistoric societies and a series of primitive ones. This historical is based on the fact that there has so far been enough cake only for a few people and that the great majority have no piece of it. Great skill is required to keep this majority from taking the cake away from these people—an attempt, incidentally, that would be pointless as long as there is nothing more to eat, since then only another minority would have its cake. By means of what is sometimes called a revolution, often only another privileged class comes to power, a class that is indeed somewhat larger but that, in the end, also keeps the majority of people away from the "cake of the world."

In order to keep the majority in line, the holders of power have to create many conditions, primarily of a psychological nature. Thus, they must teach people to obey, to subordinate themselves, to get used to placing their own interests under those of "duties," to feel sinful, to curtail their capacity for action; the holders of power have to serve the majority falsehoods that are supposed to explain why everything is proceeding justly, and to keep them from critically analyzing social problems.

Yet a society is conceivable that, as Marx said, functions rationally and in harmony with the dignity of man, that is *transparent,* that is organized on the basis of an insight into the resources at hand and possible development, a society in which it is no longer necessary to feed people false ideologies. In it, man can see clearly and is not forced to be unreasonable. In this case, one must bear in mind that reason is the most important thing that man qua man possesses.   Interview with Reif, pp. 41–43.

The alternative of *having* versus *being* does not appeal to common sense. To have, so it would seem, is a normal function of our life: in order to live we must have things. Moreover, we must have things in order to enjoy them. In a culture in which the supreme goal is to have—and to have more and more—and in which one can speak of someone as "being worth a million dollars," how can there be an alternative between having and being? On the contrary, it would seem that the very essence of being is having; that if one *has* nothing, one *is* nothing.

Yet the great Masters of Living have made the alternative between having and being a central issue of their respective systems. The Buddha teaches that in order to arrive at the highest stage of human development, we must not crave possessions. Jesus teaches: "For whosoever will save his life shall lose it; but whosoever will lose his life for my sake, the same shall save it. For what is a man advantaged, if he gain the whole world, and lose himself, or be cast away?" (Luke 9:24–25). Meister Eckhart taught that to have nothing and make oneself open and "empty," not to let one's ego stand in one's way, is the condition for achieving spiritual wealth and strength. Marx taught that luxury is as much a vice as poverty and that our goal should be to *be* much, not to *have* much.

For many years I had been deeply impressed by this distinction and was seeking its empirical basis in the concrete study of individuals and groups by the psychoanalytic method. What I saw has led me to conclude that this distinction, together with that between love of life and love of the dead, represents the most crucial problem of existence; that empirical anthropological and psychoanalytic data tend to demonstrate that *having and being are two fundamental modes of experience, the respective strength of which determine the differences between the characters of individuals and various types of social character.*   *To Have Or to Be?*, pp. 15–16.

In contemporary society the having mode of existing is assumed to be rooted in human nature and, hence, virtually unchangeable. The same idea is expressed in the dogma that people are basically lazy, passive by nature, and that they do not want to work or to do anything else, unless they are driven by the incentive of material gain . . . or hunger . . . or the fear of punishment. This dogma is doubted by hardly anybody, and it determines our methods of education and of work. But it is little more than an expression of the wish to prove the value of our social arrangements by imputing to them that they follow the needs of human nature. To the members of many different societies of both past and present, the concept of innate human selfishness and laziness would appear as fantastic as the reverse sounds to us.

The truth is that both the having and the being modes of existence are potentialities of human nature, that our biological urge for survival tends to further the having mode, but that selfishness and laziness are not the only propensities inherent in human beings.

We human beings have an inherent and deeply rooted desire to be: to express our faculties, to be active, to be related to others, to escape the prison cell of selfishness. The truth of this statement is proven by so much evidence that a whole volume could easily be filled with it. D. O. Hebb has formulated the gist of the problem in the most general form by stating that *the only behavioral problem is to account for inactivity, not for activity.* [Cf. E. Fromm, 1991b, pp. 145–97.]

These considerations seem to indicate that both tendencies are present in human beings: the one, to *have*—to possess—that owes its strength in the last analysis to the biological factor of the desire for survival; the other, to *be*—to share, to give, to sacrifice—that owes its strength to the specific conditions of human existence and the inherent need to overcome one's isolation by oneness with others. From these two contradictory strivings in every human being it follows that the social structure, its values and norms, decides which of the two becomes dominant. Cultures that foster the greed for possession, and thus the having mode of existence, are rooted in one human potential; cultures that foster being and sharing are in the other potential. We must decide which of these potentials we want to cultivate, realizing, however, that our decision is largely determined by the socioeconomic structure of our given society that inclines us toward one or the other solution. *To Have Or to Be?*, pp. 100 and 105–6.

Both modes of experience are to be found in almost everybody: Rare are those who do not experience having at all, far more numerous are those for whom it is almost the only experience they know. Most people are characterized by the particular blending of the having and being modes in their character structure. *The Art of Being*, p. 106.

This preliminary survey of the meaning of having and being leads to these conclusions:

(1) By *being* or *having* I do not refer to certain separate qualities of a subject as illustrated in such statements as "I have a car" or "I am white" or "I am happy." I refer to two fundamental modes of existence, to two different kinds of orientation toward self and the world, to two different kinds of character structure the respective predominance of which determines the totality of a person's thinking, feeling, and acting.

(2) In the having mode of existence my relationship to the world is one of possessing and owning, one in which I want to make everybody and everything, including myself, my property.

(3) In the being mode of existence, we must identify two forms of being. One is in contrast to *having,* the other form of being is in contrast to *appearing* and refers to the true nature, the true reality, of a person or a thing in contrast to deceptive appearances. *To Have Or to Be?*, p. 24.

The Nature of the Having Mode of Existence

The sentence "I have something" expresses the relation between the subject, *I* (or he, we , you, they), and the object,

O. It implies that the subject is permanent and the object is permanent. But is there permanence in the subject? Or in the object? I shall die; I may lose the social position that guarantees my having something. The object is similarly not permanent: it can be destroyed, or it can be lost, or it can lose its value. Speaking of having something permanently rests upon the illusion of a permanent and indestructible substance. If I seem to have everything, I have—in reality—nothing, since my having, possessing, controlling an object is only a transitory moment in the process of living.

In the last analysis, the statement "*I* [subject] have *0* [object]" expresses a definition of *I* through my possession of *0*. The subject is not *myself* but *I am what I have*. My property constitutes myself and my identity. The underlying thought in the statement "I am I" is "*I am I because I have X*" —*X* equaling all natural objects and persons to whom I relate myself through my power to control them, to make them permanently mine.

In the having mode, there is no alive relationship between me and what I have. It and I have become things, and I have *it*, because I have the force to make it mine. But there is also a reverse relationship: *it has me,* because my sense of identity, i.e., of sanity, rests upon my having *it* (and as many things as possible). The having mode of existence is not established by an alive, productive process between subject and object; it makes *things* of both object and subject. The relationship is one of deadness, not aliveness.

To Have Or to Be?, pp. 77–78.

An important distinction is that between property for use (functional property), and property for possession (nonfunctional), although there are many blendings of these two types. In German the difference between the two kinds of properties is made clear by the use of two different words: *Besitz* and *Eigentum*. *Besitz* comes from *sitzen,* and means literally that upon which one sits; it refers to that which one controls, legally and factually, but it is not related to one's own productive action. *Eigentum,* on the other hand, is different. While *aig* is the Germanic root of *haben* (to have), it has changed its meaning in the course of many centuries so that Meister Eckhart could translate it already in the thirteenth century as the German equivalent of the Latin word for property *(proprietas). Proper* corresponds to *eigen;* it means that which is particular of a person (as in "proper name"). *Eigentum = proprietas = property* refers then, to all that is particular of a person as a specific individual: his own body, the things that he uses daily, and to which he gives some of his individuality by this daily acquaintance, even his tools and abode—all that forms his constant surroundings.

Man cannot exist without "having," but he can exist very well with purely *functional* having and has existed so for the first 40,000 years of his history since he emerged as *homo sapiens.* Indeed, he can only exist sanely if he has mainly functional property and a minimum of dead property.

Functional property is an existential and actual need of man. It is clear that I can own no more than I can reasonably use. This coupling of owning and using has several consequences: (1) My activity is constantly stimulated, because having only what I use, I am constantly stimulated to be active; (2) The greediness to possess (avarice) can hardly develop, because I can only wish to have the amount of things that fit my capacity to use them productively; (3) I can hardly develop envy since it would be useless to envy another for what he has when I am busy using what I have; and (4) I am not worried by the fear of losing what I have, since functional property is easily replaceable.

Nonfunctional, institutional possession is an entirely different experience. It satisfies a pathological need, conditioned by certain socioeconomic circumstances.

Everybody must have a body, shelter, tools, weapons, vessels. These things are necessary for his biological existence; there are other things that he needs for his spiritual existence, such as ornaments and objects of decoration— briefly, artistic and "sacred" objects and the means to produce them. They can be property in the sense that an individual uses them exclusively, but they are functional property.

With an increase in civilization, functional property in things increases. The individual may have several suits or dresses, a house, labor-saving devices, radio and television sets, record players and recordings, books, tennis rackets, a pair of skis. . . . All these possessions need not be different from those functional possessions that exist in primitive cultures. They need not be, but they often are. The change of function happens at the point where possession ceases to be an instrument for greater aliveness and productivity but is transformed into a means for passive-receptive consumption.   *The Art of Being,* pp. 103 and 106.

Much of the moral and political discussion has centered on the question: To have or not to have? On the moral-religious level this meant the alternative between ascetic life and the nonascetic life, the latter including both productive enjoyment and unlimited pleasure. This alternative loses most of its meaning if one's emphasis is not *on* the single act of behavior but on the attitude underlying it. Ascetic behavior, with its constant preoccupation with nonenjoyment, may be only the negation of strong desires for having and consuming. In the ascetic theses desires can be repressed, yet in the very attempt to suppress having and consuming, the person may be equally preoccupied with having and consuming. This denial by overcompensation is, as psychoanalytic data show, very frequent. It occurs in such cases as fanatical vegetarians repressing destructive impulses, fanatical antiabortionists repressing their murderous impulses, fanatics of "virtue" repressing their own "sinful" impulses. What matters here is not a certain conviction as such, but the fanaticism that supports it. This, like all fanaticism, suggests the suspicion that it serves to cover other, and usually the opposite, impulses.

To Have Or to Be?, p. 84.

Having and Possessiveness

The norms by which society functions also mold the character of its members (social character). In an industrial society these are: the wish to acquire property, to keep it, and to increase it, i.e., to make a profit, and those who own property are admired and envied as superior beings. But the vast majority of people own no property in a real sense of capital and capital goods, and the puzzling question arises: How can such people fulfill or even cope with their passion for acquiring and keeping property, or how can they feel like owners of property when they have no property to speak of?

Of course, the obvious answer is that even people who are property poor own *something*—and they cherish their little possessions as much as the owners of capital cherish their property. And like the big property owners, the poor are obsessed by the wish to preserve what they do have and to increase it, even though by an infinitesimal amount (for instance by saving a penny here, two cents there).

Perhaps the greatest enjoyment is not so much in owning material things but in owning living beings [in owning themselves, values and ideals]. The answer lies in extending the area of ownership to include friends, lovers, health, travel, art objects, God, one's own ego. A brilliant picture of the bourgeois obsession with property is given by Max Stirner. Persons are transformed into things; their relations to each other assume the character of ownership. "Individualism," which in its positive sense means liberation from social chains, means, in the negative sense, "self-ownership," the right—and the duty—to invest one's energy in the success of one's own person.

Our ego is the most important object of our property feeling, for it comprises many things: our body, our name, our social status, our possessions (including our knowledge), the image we have of ourselves and the image we want others to have of us. Our ego is a mixture of real qualities, such as knowledge and skills, and of certain fictitious qualities that we build around a core of reality. But the essential point is not so much what the ego's content is, but that the ego is felt as a thing we each possess, and that this "thing" is the basis of our sense of identity.

The most important factor lies in the change in social character that has occurred during the past century and a half, i.e., from the "hoarding" to the "marketing" character. Although the change does not do away with the having orientation, it does modify it considerably. The proprietary feeling also shows up in other relationships, for example toward doctors, dentists, lawyers, bosses, workers. People express it in speaking of "*my* doctor," "*my* dentist," "*my* workers," and so on.

But aside from their property attitude toward other human beings, people experience an unending number of objects, even feelings, as property. Take health and illness, for example. People who discuss their health do so with a proprietary feeling, referring to *their* sicknesses, *their* operations, *their* treatments—*their* diets, *their* medicines. They clearly consider that health and sickness are property; their property relationship to their bad health is analogous, say, to that of a stockholder whose shares are losing part of their original value in a badly falling market.

Ideas and beliefs can also become property, as can even habits. For instance, anyone who eats an identical breakfast at the same time each morning can be disturbed by even a slight change in that routine, because his habit has become a property whose loss endangers his security.

A helpful approach to understanding the mode of having is to recall one of Freud's most significant findings, that after going through their infant phase of mere passive receptivity followed by a phase of aggressive exploitative receptivity, all children, before they reach maturity, go through a phase Freud designated the *anal-erotic.* Freud discovered that this phase often remains dominant during a person's development, and that when it does it leads to the development of the *anal character,* i.e., the character of a person whose main energy in life is directed toward having, saving, and hoarding money, and material things as well as feelings, gestures, words, and energy.

To Have Or to Be?, pp. 73–74 and 83.

Freud discovered that there is a relation between the stingy, punctual, orderly, and excessively clean behavior, on the one hand, and certain events in a person's early development, such as his toilet training, on the other hand. Children who have already learned to relieve themselves properly at an early or precocious age develop an anal character, in which, according to Freud, is the result of the pressure that is exerted on the libido during the anal phase.

I do not think that this causal relationship is correct. I do not believe that these events with respect to the anal zone lead to such a character formation. Rather, both elements run parallel: in the case of people who develop this character, environmental influences also play a role next to innate factors. It is quite true that the parents' conduct with respect to their children's toilet training has a big influence on this, but mothers who are so bent on the cleanliness of their children are quite fanatical not only on this point, but they themselves have a retentive character. For them, everything that has to do with the evacuation of the bowels—defecation, digestion, constipation, etc.—is of the greatest interest. It is the favorite subject of their thoughts, and they like to talk about it when they find the opportunity. For them, the most important thing in life is how much a person has, how much a person saves, how much a person holds in reserve, how much a person spends or should not spend. Yet the influence of the mother on the development of her child is a much more extensive one, and the influence on the anal zone represents only one of the four elements in this region of influence, since the mother herself is an "agent of society."

Interview with Reif, pp. 34–37.

[The connection between the having mode of existence and anality can be demonstrated with the symbolic connection between feces and gold.] Seeking the reason for the symbolic identity of gold and feces, Freud proposes the hypothesis that their identity may be based on the very fact of their radical contrast, gold being the most precious and feces the most worthless substance known to man. Freud ignores the other possibility that gold is the most precious substance for civilization, whose economy is (generally) based on gold, but that this holds by no means for those primitive societies for which gold may not have had any great value.

More importantly, while the pattern of his society suggests that man think of gold as the most precious substance, he may unconsciously carry a notion that gold is dead, sterile (like salt), without life (except when used in jewelry); that it is amassed labor, meant to be hoarded, the foremost example of possession without function. Can one eat gold? Can one make anything grow with gold (except when it has been transformed into capital)?

This dead, sterile aspect of gold is shown in the myth of King Midas. He was so avaricious that his wish was granted that everything he touched became gold. Eventually, he had to die precisely because one cannot live from gold. In this myth is a clear vision of the sterility of gold, and it is by no means the highest value, as Freud assumed. Freud was too much a son of his time to be aware of the negative value of money and possession and, hence, of the critical implications of his concept of the anal character.

The Art of Being, pp. 109–10.

The Nature of the Being Mode of Existence

Most of us know more about the mode of having than we do about the mode of being, because having is by far the more frequently experienced mode in our culture. But something more important than that makes defining the mode of being so much more difficult than defining the mode of having, namely the very nature of the difference between these two modes of existence.

Having refers to *things* and things are fixed and *describable.* Being refers to *experience,* and human experience is in principle not describable. What is fully describable is our *persona*—the mask we each wear, the ego we present—for this persona is in itself a thing. In contrast, the living human being is not a dead image and cannot be described like a thing. In fact, the living human being cannot be described at all. Indeed, much can be said about me, about my character, about my total orientation to life. This insightful knowledge can go very far in understanding and describing my own or another's psychical structure. But the total me, my whole individuality, my *suchness* that is as unique as my fingerprints, can never be fully understood, not even by empathy, for no two human beings are entirely alike. Only in the process of mutual alive-relatedness can the other and I overcome the barrier of separateness, inasmuch as we both participate in the dance of life. Yet our full identification of each other can never be achieved.

The mode of being has as its prerequisites independence, freedom, and the presence of critical reason. Its fundamental characteristic is that of being active, not in the sense of outward activity, of busyness, but of inner activity, the productive use of our human powers. To be active means to give expression to one's faculties, talents, to the wealth of human gifts with which—though in varying degrees— every human being is endowed. It means to renew oneself, to grow, to flow out, to love, to transcend the prison of one's isolated ego, to be interested, to "list," [a Middle English term] to give. Yet none of these experiences can be fully expressed in words. The words are vessels that are filled with experience that overflows the vessels. The words point to an experience; they are not the experience. The moment that I express what I experience exclusively in thought and words, the experience has gone: it has dried up, is dead, a mere thought. Hence being is indescribable in words and is communicable only by sharing my experience. In the structure of having, the dead word rules; in the structure of being, the alive and inexpressible experience rules. (Of course, in the being mode there is also thinking that is alive and productive.)

Perhaps the being mode may best be described in a symbol suggested to me by [the Swiss glass painter] Max Hunziger: A blue glass appears to be blue when light shines through it because it absorbs all other colors and thus does not let them pass. This is to say, we call a glass "blue" precisely because it does not retain the blue waves. It is named not for what it possesses but for what it gives out.

To Have Or to Be?, pp. 89–91.

Being is the activity of humans, indeed, it is *human* activity, which does not mean activity as such: dragging stones from here to there and then dragging them back again is not work in a human sense. The being mode of existence means to be living, to be interested, to see things, to see people, to listen to people, to put oneself in the place of others, to put oneself in one's own place, to make life interesting, to make something beautiful of life.

Interview with Ferrari, pp. 60–61.

Being and Productivity

Man is not only a rational and social animal; he can also be defined as a producing animal, capable of transforming the materials that he finds at hand, using his reason and imagination. Not only *can* he produce, he *must* produce in order to live. Material production, however, is but the most frequent expression of or symbol for productiveness as an aspect of character. The productive orientation of personality refers to a fundamental attitude, a *mode of relatedness* in all realms of human experience. It covers physical, mental, emotional, and sensory responses to others, to oneself, and to things.

Productiveness is man's ability to use his powers and to realize the potentialities inherent in him. Saying *he* uses *his* powers implies that he must be free and not dependent on someone who controls his powers. It implies, furthermore, that he is guided by reason, since he can make use of his powers only if he knows what they are, how to use them, and what to use them for. Productiveness means that he experiences himself as the embodiment of his powers and as the "actor," that he feels himself as the subject of his powers, that he is not alienated from his powers, i.e., that they are not masked from him and transferred to an idolized object, person, or institution.

Another way of describing productiveness (and like any other experience, it cannot be defined but rather it must be described in such a way that others who share the experience know what one is talking about) is to say that the productive person animates that which he touches. He gives soul to that which surrounds him. (It is fortunate that the black radical movement has brought the concept of soul out of its disrepute by using it to mean a quality of animated activity rather than its traditional use as a metaphysical concept.)

The productive person gives birth to his own faculties and give life to persons and to things. By his own productive approach, he calls forth a productive response in others unless they are so unproductive that they cannot be touched. One might say that the productive person sensitizes both himself and others, and is sensitive to himself and to the world around him. This sensitivity exists in the realms of thinking and feeling. What matters in the productive attitude is not its particular object, which may be people, nature, or things, but rather the whole approach. The productive orientation is rooted in the love of life (biophilia—cf. E. Fromm, 1964a). It is *being,* not *having.*

Social Character in a Mexican Village, pp. 71–72.

The productive person who is oriented toward being is active from within. He has an active relationship with the world. For him, relatedness and connectedness with the world is an inner necessity. The person who is oriented toward being is the person who constantly changes during the course of his life and who does not remain the same in every action that he performs, but for whom, quite to the contrary, every action simultaneously means a change of his person. In this case, a person is no longer an ultimate, isolated entity in the Cartesian sense, such as physicists before Einstein believed that the atom was the ultimate unit of matter. Instead, man by his nature is located in a process of comprehending and understanding the world, of being interested in the world—if we consider "interest" in its original etymological sense of inter-esse, of being-within—a process by which the division between a rigid subject and an equally rigid, externally located object is overcome in favor of the idea of a constant relationship in which (as the Buddhists say) "I do not only see the rose, the rose also sees me." This is just a special formulation of this procedural, reciprocal relationship of man to the world.

There is more: this being-in-the-world, this giving-oneself-to-the-world, this self-transformation in the act of life, is only possible when man loses his greediness and stinginess and abandons his self as an isolated, fixed ego that stands opposed to the world. Only when man abandons this self, when he can empty himself (to use the language of mystics), only then can he fill himself entirely. For he must be empty of his egotistical self in order to become full of what comes to him from the world. It does not matter whether that something is a person or nature or an idea. The person who is filled up with himself is neither open nor free to give himself. To quote Marx once again: The rich man is the one who is much, and not the one who has

much. In the twentieth century, we could perhaps add: nor the person who consumes much!
"The Problems of Surplus," pp. 325–26.

[The relevance of being related in a productive, being oriented way] can be demonstrated by the question: What is the source of energy from which we live? You might say there is one source of energy that is purely physical, which is rooted in the chemistry of our body, and we know that that energy is on the decline after the age of twenty-five. After that, we are slowly running down, as far as that source of energy is concerned.

But there is another source of energy that springs from our being related to the world, our being concerned. You can experience it sometimes when you are with somebody whom you love, or when you read something that is intensely interesting, exciting. Then you don't get tired. You feel energy coming up that is unexpected. You feel a deep sense of joy, and if you watch some people at the age of eighty who have lived a life of intense relatedness, love, concern, interest actually, you will see the surprising and overwhelming fact of a freshness and an energy there that has nothing to do with the body chemistry, with the sources they have at their disposal.

Joy, energy, happiness, all this depends on the degree to which we are related, to which we are concerned, and that is to say, to which we are in touch with the reality of our feelings, with the reality of other people, and not to experience them as abstractions that we can look at like the commodities at the market. Secondly, in this process of being related, we experience ourselves as entities, as I, who is related to the world. I become one with the world in my relatedness to the world, but I also experience myself as a self, as an individuality, as something unique, because in this process of relatedness, I am at the same time the subject of this activity, of this process, of relating myself. I am I and I am the other person but I am I too. I become one with the object of my concern, but in this process, I experience myself also as a subject.

The Pathology of Normalcy, pp. 75–76.

Man needs an object for the expression of his faculties ("Wesenskraft"); that his essential powers are endowed with the dynamic quality of having to strive for an object they can relate to and unite themselves with. *The dynamism of human nature is primarily rooted in this need of man to express his faculties toward the world, rather than in his need to use the world as a means for the satisfaction of his physiological necessities.* What Marx is saying is that because I have eyes I have the need to see; because I have ears I have the need to hear; because I have a brain I have the need to think; and because I have a heart I have the need to feel. In short, because I am man, I am in need of man and of the world. In this state of experience, the separation of subject from object disappears, they become unified by the bond of human active relatedness to the object.

On Being Human, p. 156.

Essentials of a Life
Between Having and Being

Consumerism (as a Compensation of
Anxiety and Depression) versus
the Joy of Life

*M*an is in the process of becoming a *homo consumens,* a total consumer. This image of man almost has the character of a new religious vision in which heaven is just a big warehouse where everyone can buy something new every day, indeed, where he can buy everything that he wants and even a little more than his neighbor. This vision of the total consumer is indeed a new image of man that is conquering the world, quite regardless of differences of political organization and ideology.

To begin with, I would like to describe this *homo consumens* as a psychological phenomenon, as a new type of social character, which has its own dynamic. This dynamic can be understood only in the sense of the Freudian character dynamic if one distinguishes between what a person is aware of and the unconscious forces that drive him. *Homo consumens* is the person for whom everything becomes an object of consumption: cigarettes and beer, liquor, books, love and sexuality, lectures and picture galleries.

There is nothing whatsoever that could not become an object of consumption for this person. Even certain drugs from which one can derive immediate enlightenment are consumed.

The question arises: Is not man by his nature someone who must consume in order to stay alive? Indeed, man must consume things just like any other living creature. Yet the novel phenomenon consists in the fact that a character structure develops for which even things that were acquired in an entirely different manner, i.e, the rich world of human invention and culture, become, without exception, objects of consumption.

From a psychological point of view, what does this manner of consumption consist in [and what is used to compensate for it]? Unconsciously, this new type of person is a passive, empty, anxious, isolated person for whom life has no meaning and who is profoundly alienated and bored. If one asks these people who are today consuming liquor, travel vacations, and books whether they feel unhappy and bored, then they answer, "Not at all, we're completely happy. We go on trips, we drink, we eat, we buy more and more for ourselves. You aren't bored doing that!"

Consciously, then, these people are not bored. At this point, one must indeed ask analytically whether it is possible that these people are perhaps unconsciously empty, bored, and alienated and whether it is possible that they are passive people unconsciously—the eternal infant who does not only wait for his bottle, but for whom everything is a bottle and who never develops an activity by his own powers.

In fact, the anxious, bored, alienated person compensates for his anxiety by a compulsive consumption that, as a general illness—or, more precisely, as a sympton of the "pathology of normalcy"—no one thinks is an illness. Indeed, one thinks of the idea of "illness" only when someone is sicker than other people. When, however everyone suffers from the same illness, the idea of illness does not at all arise in people's minds. Thus, this inner void, this inner anxiety is symbolically cured by compulsive consumption. Compulsive eating disorder is the paradigm of this mechanism. If one looks into why certain people suffer from compulsive eating disorders, then one indeed finds that, behind this disorder, which is acknowledged as such, there is something unconscious, namely, depression or anxiety. A person feels empty, and in order simultaneously to fill this void symbolically, he fills himself up with other things, with things that come from the outside, in order to overcome the feeling of inner emptiness and inner weakness. Many people notice in themselves that, when they are anxious or feel depressed, they have a certain tendency to buy something or to go to the refrigerator or to eat a little more than usual and that they then feel somewhat less depressed and somewhat less anxious.

On the other hand, the problem is very closely tied up with the economic structure of modern western society, which is economically based on the reality of complete, absolute and ever-growing consumption. What the economy needs most of all for its own operation is that people buy, buy, and buy again, since there is otherwise no constantly growing demand for goods that industry can produce and must produce to an ever-growing degree if it wants to multiply its capital. For that reason, industry compels people by all means of temptation to consume more.

In the nineteenth century, it was immoral to buy something for which one did not have the money. In the twentieth century, it is considered to be immoral not to buy something for which one does not have the money, since people buy and travel even on installment payments. By means of an enormously refined advertising mechanism, the economy seduces people into buying more and more.

People become anxious and alienated by the capitalist system's method of production: because this system produces larger and larger economic and bureaucratic giants vis-à-vis which the individual person feels small and helpless; because the individual person can participate less and less actively in the events within society; because there is an enormous fear in many social circles of not moving up, of losing the position that one has attained, the fear that one's own wife and friends will judge one as a "failure" if one does not reach what the others reach.

In reality, we are dealing with a *circulus vitiosus:* the person who becomes anxious in this system consumes. But also the person who is lured to consumption becomes anxious, because he becomes a passive person, because he always only takes things in, because he does not actively experience anything in the world. The more anxious he becomes, the more he must consume, and the more he consumes, the more anxious he becomes. Thus, there arises the circle in which man feels all the more powerless as his machines become more powerful, that is, as what he produces becomes more powerful. And he compensates for all this by constant and never-ending consumption.

The problem of *pseudo-freedom* is tied up with the problem of consumption. In the nineteenth century, the idea of freedom was essentially connected with having property at one's disposal and with the freedom of commercial enterprise. Today, private property is only a very small part of the means of production in the advanced capitalist countries. General Motors and the Ford Company, the two largest automobile giants in America, for example, are in the hands of a self-perpetuating bureaucracy, and the hundreds of thousands of owners of the actual property do not have a crucial influence on the companies. (The freedom of property is a concept that was really meaningful only in the nineteenth century. That is why Marx was wrong when he believed that one could change something essential through the socialization of the means of production. Marx oriented himself to the nineteenth century's concept of property and did not foresee that property as a means of production would no longer be a basic notion in the twentieth century.)

Today's pseudo-freedom lies in the sphere of consumption. The consumer comes to the supermarket and sees ten different brands of cigarettes that have already been trumpeted on the radio, on television, and in the newspapers. They all are vying for his favor, as if they wanted to say, "Please, choose me!" Now, it is true that the buyer basically knows that all these are actually the same brands, whether they be cigarettes or the soaps that are praised with pretty girls or even just with girls' legs. Purely intellectually, the buyer is aware that all of that is completely irrational. Nevertheless, it gives him a feeling of freedom to be able to choose what he wants. So he grants his favor to Chesterfield cigarettes instead of Marlboro or to Marlboro instead of Chesterfield.

By exactly this means, though, he becomes a pseudo-personality. When he defines himself by smoking Marlboro, he determines his being by having this object of consumption. That is his self, his personality. In the act of choosing, he experiences his power, while, in reality, he is experiencing his powerlessness, because his choosing is only the result of influences that are at work behind his back. He believes that he is consciously making his choice, while, in reality, he is prompted into choosing between two different products that are suggested to him. It is important that people smoke and that, in making this choice, they have the experience of freedom and of power.

"Problems of Surplus," pp. 318–21.

There is a certain sickness in this drive for ever-increasing consumption and the danger is that by being filled with a need for consumption the person does not really solve the problem of inner passivity, of inner vacuity, of anxiety, of being depressed because life in some way doesn't make sense. The Old Testament says that the worst sin of the Hebrews was that they had lived without joy in the midst of plenty (cf. Dtn 28, 47). I am afraid the critics of our society could also say that we live with much fun and excitement but with little joy in the midst of plenty.

Problems of Aging, p. 11.

The concept of *happiness* is also tied to consumption. If one were to treat this topic philosophically, one would have to go back to the essence and the psychology of the Enlightenment. Yet if one asks people today what actually makes them happy, then you hear the answer, "It would make us happy if we could afford everything that we want." The popular concept of happiness that most people probably have today is that not only is freedom founded on consumption, but so is happiness and that the only thing standing in the way of freedom and happiness is the fact that they do not have enough money to consume everything that they would like to consume.

"Problems of Surplus," p. 321.

But consumption does not make people happy, even if most people believe that they would be happier if their level of consumption were higher. Many studies as well as simple observation show that that is so. Man becomes happy through the engagement of his own powers and by actively experiencing himself in the world. Man's happiness lies in his love of life, and that is something very active: in the *joy* arising from a plant, from a landscape, from music, from

everything by means of which man can use his given abilities—which are partially natural and partially cultural—to create something. If he cannot do that, then, as far as I can see, his feeling of happiness is mistaken. He convinces himself, and he is convinced by others, that he is happy.
                                    Interview with Lodemann, pp. 67–68.

Only inner productivity is accompanied by *joy*. External productivity, i.e., making something, does not bring joy. On the contrary. Indeed, this is the tragedy, namely, that man makes many things—goods, machines—but does not experience any joy in doing so, but, quite to the contrary, feels like a prisoner. Interview with Reif 1977, p. 35.

Joy is the concomitant of productive activity. It is not a "peak experience," which culminates and ends suddenly, but rather a plateau, a feeling state that accompanies the productive expression of one's essential human faculties. Joy is not the ecstatic fire of the moment. Joy is the glow that accompanies being. Pleasure and thrill are conducive to sadness after the so-called peak has been reached; for the thrill has been experienced, but the vessel has not grown. One's inner powers have not increased.

As is to be expected, joy must play a central role in those religious and philosophical systems that proclaim being as the goal of life. The Hebrew Bible and the later Jewish tradition, while warning against the pleasures that spring from the satisfaction of cupidity, see in joy the mood that accompanies being. The Book of Psalms ends with the group of fifteen psalms that are one great hymn of joy, and the dynamic psalms begin in fear and sadness and end in joy and gladness. The Sabbath is the day of joy, and in the Messianic Time joy will be the prevailing mood. The prophetic literature abounds with the expression of joy. Joy is considered so fundamental that, according to Talmudic law, the mourning for a close relative, whose death occurred less than a week earlier, must be interrupted by the joy of Sabbath. The Hassidic movement, whose motto, "Serve God with joy," was a verse from the Psalms, created a form of living in which joy was one of the outstanding elements. Sadness and depression were considered sins of spiritual error, if not outright sin.

In the Christian development even the name of the gospels—*Glad* Tidings—shows the central place of gladness and joy. In the New Testament, joy is the fruit of giving up having, while sadness is the mood of the one who hangs onto possessions. (See, for instance, Matthew 13:44 and 19:22.) In many of Jesus' utterances joy is conceived as a concomitant of living in the mode of being. In his last speech to the Apostles, Jesus tells of joy in the final form: "These things I have spoken to you, that my joy be in you, and that your joy may be full" (John 15:11). Joy, then, is what we experience in the process of growing nearer to the goal of becoming ourself. *To Have Or to Be?*, pp. 117–19.

Busyness (as a Compensation of Passiveness) versus Productive Activity

[That *activity* corresponds with the being mode but *passivity* is typical for the having mode of existence] is confusing for the modern mind because in our usage activity is usually defined as behavior that brings about a change in an existing situation by an expenditure of energy; it is synonymous with *being "busy."* In contrast, a person is described as passive if he is unable to change or overtly influence an existing situation by an expenditure of energy and is influenced or moved by forces outside himself. This current concept of activity takes into account only the actual expenditure of energy and the change brought about by it. It does not distinguish between the underlying psychic conditions governing the activities.

An example, though an extreme one, of nonproductive "activity" is the activity of a person under hypnosis. The person in a deep hypnotic trance may have his eyes open, may walk, talk, and do things; he "acts." The general definition of activity would apply to him, since energy is spent and some change brought about. But if we consider the particular character and quality of this activity, we find that it is not really the hypnotized person who is the actor, but the hypnotist, who, by means of his suggestions, acts through him. While the hypnotic trance is an artificial state, it is an extreme but characteristic example of a situation in which a person can be active and yet not be the true actor, since his activity results from compelling forces over which he has no control.

Social Character in a Mexican Village, p. 73.

Activity in the modern sense refers only to behavior, not to the person behind the behavior. It makes no difference whether people are active because they are driven by external force, like a slave, or by internal compulsion, like a person driven by anxiety. It does not matter whether they are interested in their work, like a carpenter or a creative writer, or a scientist or a gardener; or whether they have no inner relation to and satisfaction in what they are doing, like the worker on the assembly line or the postal clerk.

The modern sense of activity makes no distinction between *activity* and mere *busyness.* But there is a fundamental difference between the two that corresponds to the terms "alienated" and "nonalienated" in respect to activities. In alienated activity I do not experience myself as the acting subject of my activity; rather, I experience the *outcome* of my activity—and that as something "over there," separated from me and standing above and against me. In alienated activity I do not really act; I am *acted upon* by external or internal forces. I have become separated from the result of my activity. The best observable case of alienated activity in the field of psychopathology is that of compulsive-obsessional persons. Forced by an inner urge to do something against their own wills—such as counting steps, repeating certain phrases, performing certain private rituals—they can be extremely active in the pursuit of this aim; but as psychoanalytic investigation has amply shown, they are driven by an inner force of which they are unaware. An equally clear example of alienated activity is posthypnotic behavior. People under hypnotic suggestion to do this or that upon awakening from the hypnotic trance will do these things without any awareness that they are not doing what they want to do, but are following their respective hypnotists' previously given orders.

In nonalienated activity, I experience *myself* as the *subject* of my activity. Nonalienated activity is a process of giving birth to something, of producing something and remaining related to what I produce. This also implies that my activity is a manifestation of my powers, that I and my activity and the result of my activity are one. I call this nonalienated activity *productive activity*.

"Productive" as used here does not refer to the capacity to create something new or original, as an artist or scientist may be creative. Neither does it refer to the product of my activity, but to its quality. A painting or a scientific treatise may be quite unproductive, i.e., sterile; on the other hand, the process going on in persons who are aware of themselves in depth, or who truly "see" a tree rather than just look at it, or who read a poem and experience in themselves the movement of feelings the poet has expressed in words—that process may be very productive, although nothing is "produced." Productive activity denotes the state of inner activity; it does not necessarily have a connection with the creation of a work of art, of science, or of something "useful." Productiveness is a character orientation all human beings are capable of, to the extent that they are not emotionally crippled. Productive persons animate whatever they touch. They give birth to their own faculties and bring life to other persons and to things. "Activity" and "passivity" can each have two entirely different meanings. Alienated activity, in the sense of mere busyness, is actually "passivity," in the sense of productivity; while passivity, in terms of nonbusyness, may be nonalienated activity. This is so difficult to understand today because most activity is alienated "passivity," while productive passivity is rarely experienced.   *To Have Or to Be?*, pp. 88–90.

An activity can be done in order to avoid boredom, or something is done out of relatedness or concern with something. You can observe or sense the different. You have spent an evening with friends, and you have talked for the whole evening. Try to watch how you feel when you leave. Do you feel happy, alive, pleasant, good, or do you feel kind of tired and bored, or not even bored but a little bit dissatisfied and depressed? You just have the feeling, "Well, all right. Thank God I can go to bed now." Or is it quite different: Where you have been with somebody and haven't gotten tired, and even if it is late you have enjoyed yourself. You feel alive. You feel kind of happy. Then you know that what you have been doing is not just to avoid boredom.

The Pathology of Normalcy, p. 76.

To cite a simple example of the difference between activity that is oriented toward having or toward being: Imagine that you see a lake and then say about this lake at a distance: "There is a lake. There is water." And then just imagine that you have jumped into the lake and have swum around in it. Your statement, "There's water over there," is now an entirely different one. True, even then you are not the water. But you are also not not the water, because you are in the water, because you are wet and your relationship to the water is one of constant process.

The concept of being active in a manner that is oriented toward being can be explained by the following example: If, for example, you simply lie on the water and float, then that is an active process, although it looks entirely passive, since a person who cannot swim, also cannot passively float because he does not have control over the delicate balance that is necessary to float. So, whether you "become wet" with your things or "stay dry" determines—to put it figuratively—the difference in your relationship to the thing. How you talk with a person, how you look at a landscape, how you think a thought, this determines the difference between a static, egoistical and isolated person and a developing and active person who is in the world.

"Problems of Surplus," pp. 325–26.

Destructiveness (as a Compensation of Boredom) versus Creativity

Boredom is one of the most terrible torments. Pain is often less distressing than boredom. Boredom comes from the fact that man has become purely an instrument, that he cultivates no initiative, that he feels not responsible, that he feels like a little cog in a machine that someone could replace with another at any time.

Boredom also arises from the fact that man is a completely alienated human being, alienated from himself, from other people, from work and from the fact that man faces a world over which he no longer has any control and in which, for this reason, his interest also perpetually wanes. This is true not only of workers, but also of white-collar workers and of most people in general, with the exception of those who have a profession that is really interesting and that allows them to fashion and to experience their own agency productively. This is sometimes the case with scientists, scholars, doctors, and top managers who, when they are at the head of a company, actually can do something creative, although they, too, are ultimately white-collar workers who have superiors and are subject to the laws of the maximization of profit.

A person is happy only when he is interested in what he is doing; only then does he feel that the power of his own being is confirmed; only then can he express that power; only then is he not isolated; and only then does he feel connected with the world and not powerless. He can love things, he can love his work and he can love people. Yet if he is nothing but a tiny part of a machine, if he does nothing but carry out orders—it does not at all matter whether he is paid well for doing this—if he has no real power to act, if he shows no interest because there is nothing interesting for him to do, then he becomes bored.

The person who suffers from boredom can hardly bear it. He tries to compensate for it—through consumption. He drives around in his car, he drinks and he does this and that so that he can somehow "spend" two, three hours during which he does not have to toil strenuously at the workplace. He does indeed save time with his machines, but after he has saved time, then he does not know what to do with it. Then he is embarrassed and tries to kill this saved time in a respectable way. To a large extent, our entertainment industry, our parties and leisure activities are nothing but an attempt to do away with the boredom of waiting in a respectable manner.

But boredom is hardly purged from the world in this manner. The bored person who cannot experience anything positive has yet another way to experience intensity: destruction. If I destroy life, then I feel a sensation of superiority over life, I take revenge on it because I have not succeeded in giving meaning to life. By taking revenge and destroying, I prove to myself that life has not, in fact, cheated me. I can not bear the fact that other people enjoy life and that they have it better because they are alive while I face life coldly and lifelessly.

There is a great deal of clinical material about the desire to destroy. I am thinking, for example, about the many cases in the United States where young people simply go out and stab to death a person whom they do not know at all and then say, "That was the greatest moment of my life, because I saw in this person's agonized, twisted face that I really can make a mark, that I am not a complete nothing."

Now, it seems to me that destructive tendencies today are increasing so tremendously quickly because boredom is increasing, because the meaninglessness of life is increasing, because people are becoming more anxious, and because they have no faith in the future and no hope. And not least because man feels deceived by all promises, all ideologies, all political parties, and all religions. In this situation of feeling deceived, many people see only a single gratification as a way out: namely, to destroy life itself in order to justify themselves and their own failure.

The necrophilic desire to destroy is something different from sadism, although both are very often intertwined with one another, which is nothing unusual in the case of two impulses. The sadist does not want to destroy his object; rather, his goal consists much more in trying to control it.

To this extent, the sadist is still relatively connected to life. His gratification is power over an object. He enjoys this control. On the other hand, the person who is motivated by a desire to destroy does not want to control, but to destroy.

Necrophilia is the love of that which is no longer alive *(nekrós)*, the state of being attracted to what is dead. People do not believe in the presence of this extremely irrational passion until they look at the clinical material. This material has to do with people for whom the destruction of living organic unities and the snuffing out of life itself give the greatest pleasure. They are attracted by everything that is sick, unhealthy, and lifeless, by everything that is dismemberment, and by everything that is hostile to life. In a wider sense, the necrophile is attracted by everything that is mechanical, because he hates everything animate and is repelled by everything animate.

Necrophilia is the opposite of *biophilia,* the love of living things. The biophile finds everything attractive that is alive, where structures come together and form a unit, everything that grows and develops, whether it be people or ideas or organization or flowers. When we say in English that this or that person "loves life," then we know what we mean by that. Sometimes people only mean by this that the person likes to eat and drink well. But sometimes we also mean a person who is a *biophile* and who experiences joy in everything that is alive and grows.

Interview with Reif 1974, pp. 87–96 passim; 99–105.

[Destructiveness as a compensation of boredom is a typical manifestation of the having mode of existence. Creativity on the other hand is typical for the being mode of existence. Both destructiveness and creativity are possible answers to the need for transcendence:] We want to transcend our creatureliness, our creature nature, and we can do it in two ways. We can create life. Women can do it anyway by nature. Men can't do it that way so they do it by ideas or all sorts of things. We can transcend life by creation.

But creation is difficult in many ways and if we cannot transcend life by creation, we can transcend life by destruction. Destroying life is just as much transcending it as creating it. Destructiveness is so to speak a secondary potentiality in man. If we cannot cope with life by creating or if we cannot transcend life by creating, we try to transcend it by destroying, and in the act of destruction we make ourselves superior to life.

"Man and Society," pp. 102–3.

In talking about *creativity,* let us first consider its two possible meanings: creativity in the sense of creating something new, something that can be seen or heard by others, such as a painting, a sculpture, a symphony, a poem, a novel, etc., or creativity as an attitude, which is the condition of any creation in the former sense but which can exist even though nothing new is created in the world of things.

The first kind of creativity, that of the artist, is conditioned by a number of factors; by talent (or, if you like, you may say also, by the genes), by study and practice, and by certain economic and social conditions that permit a person to develop his talent through study and practice. Talking about creativity [as an essential of the being mode of existence] I shall deal not with this kind of creativity but with the second, the creative attitude—or, as we might also say, with creativity as a character trait.

The condition of creativeness is the willingness to be born every day. Indeed, birth is not a single process taking place when the child leaves its fetal existence and starts to breathe by itself. This event is not even as decisive as it seem in a biological sense. Although the newborn child breathes by itself, it is just as helpless and dependent on mother after birth as it was when it formed a part of her body. Even in the sense of biological development, birth has many steps. It begins with leaving the womb; then it means leaving mother's breast, mother's lap, mother's hands. Each new ability, the ability to talk, to walk, to eat, means at the same time leaving a former state.

Man is governed by a peculiar dichotomy. He is afraid of losing the former state, which is one of certainty, and yet he wants to arrive at a new state that gives rise to the possibility of using his proper forces more freely and more completely. Man is always torn between the wish to regress to the womb and the wish to be fully born. Every act of birth requires the courage to let go of something, to let go of the womb, to let go of the breast, to let go of the lap, to let go of the hand, to let go eventually of all certainties, and to rely upon one thing only: one's own powers to be aware and to respond; that is, one's own creativity.

Another condition of creativeness is the ability to accept conflict and tension resulting from polarity, rather than to avoid them. This idea is very much in contract with the current climate of opinion, in which one attempts to avoid conflicts as much as possible. All modern education tends to spare the child the experience of conflict. Everything is made easy, everyone is tolerant. Ethical norms are leveled out in such a way that there is rare occasion to experience conflict between desire and norm. There is a general superstition that conflicts are harmful, and that hence they should be avoided. The opposite is true. Conflicts are the source of wondering, of the development of strength, of what one used to call "character."

If one avoids conflicts, one becomes a smoothly running machine, where every affect is immediately leveled off, where all desires become automatic, where all feelings be-

come flattened out. Not only are there conflicts of a personal and accidental nature, as it were; there are conflicts deeply rooted in human existence. I refer here to the conflict between the fact that, at the same time we are tied to the animal kingdom by our body, its needs, and its final destruction, we transcend the animal kingdom and nature through our self-awareness, imagination, and creativeness.
                              "The Creative Attitude," pp. 51–53.

Narcissism (as a Compensation of Selflessness) versus Productive Self-Experience

To feel a sense of self, a sense of identity, is a necessity for every human being. We would become insane if we had no such sense of self. But this sense of identity differs according to the social structure of the culture in which we live. In a primitive society, where the individual has not yet emerged as an individual, the feeling of "I" can be described in terms of "I is we." My sense of identity exists in terms of my being identified with the group. As man proceeds in the process of evolution and emerges as an individual, his sense of identity exists in terms of my being identified with the group. He as a separate individual must be able to feel "I."

There is a great deal of misunderstanding about this sense of self. There are some psychologists who believe that the sense of self is nothing but a reflection of the social role that is ascribed to him, nothing but the response to expectations others have about him. Although it is true that, empirically speaking, this is the kind of self most people in our society experience, it is nevertheless a pathological phenomenon, the result of which is deep insecurity and anxiety and a compulsion to conform. One can overcome this anxiety and compulsive conformism only by developing the sense of self that I have been discussing before, where I experience myself creatively as the originator of my acts. This, however, does not mean at all that I become egocentric or narcissistic. On the contrary, I can experience myself as "I" only in the process of my relatedness to others or, to refer to our main topic, on the basis of a creative attitude.

If I am isolated and unrelated, I am so full of anxiety that I cannot possibly have a sense of identity and of self. What I experience in this case is rather a sense of proprietorship over my person. I feel then, "My home is my castle." My property is me. All that I possess, including my knowledge, my body, my memory—this constitutes me. This is not an experience of self in the sense described above, namely, the self as agent of creative experience, this is an experience, this is an experience of self based on a sense of holding on to my person as a thing, as a possession. The person with this kind of attitude is in reality a prisoner of himself, shut in and necessarily frightened and unhappy.

In order to acquire a genuine sense of self, he has to break out of his person. He has to give up holding on to himself as a thing and begin to experience himself only in the process of creative response; paradoxically enough, if he can experience himself in this process, he loses himself. He transcends the boundaries of his own person, and at the very moment when he fells "I am" he also feels "I am you," I am one with the whole world.

"The Creative Attitude," pp. 50–51

The Freudian concept of *narcissism* adds a certain clarification: "Primary narcissism" was for Freud the phenomenon that all the infant's libido affected only the infant and not, as yet, objects outside the infant's self; he supposed that in the process of maturation, libido turned itself outwards, but that in sick states it again dissociated itself from objects and was directed back upon oneself ("secondary narcissism"). Freud's concept of narcissism was quite restricted, for it relied on libido theory and because it was applied mainly to the problems of the mentally sick. The narcissism of the "normal" individual, on the other hand, received little attention. In order to understand this "normal" narcissism, we would do better to separate it from the Freudian concept of libido and to describe it as follows. For the narcissistic individual, only what is real and important has to do with himself: with *his* body, *his* wishes, *his* thoughts; everything "outside" is apprehended sensuously and conceptually, but it remains gray and nothing but an *object of thought*. The narcissist cannot love; yet one cannot say that he loves himself, but that at most he desires himself: he is egotistic, "selfish," "full of himself." For the same reason, he cannot know himself, for he is in his own way, because he is so full of himself that neither he himself, nor the world, nor God can become the object of his knowing.

Of course, narcissism has its biological foundations: from the standpoint of self-preservation, it would seem to be a rule that one's own life is more important than that of another. This probably explains why narcissism has such strength, and why constant effort is needed to overcome it or effectively to diminish it. This diminution of narcissism is the condition of love *and* of knowledge, and the central norm common to Buddhism, Judaism, and Christianity that they have spoken about under various titles.

"Religion and Religiousness," pp. 150–51

Actually, the narcissistic person is simply not capable of conceiving the world emotionally in its own reality over there. If he didn't, he would be insane. But he does not perceive it emotionally. He perceives it intellectually. I stress this point, because in regard to narcissism, as Freud used this term and also I use it, there is a confusion. Narcissism is quite different from *egotism* and vanity. A person can be very egotistical—and you might say that egotism always implies also a certain amount of narcissism, but not necessarily more than the average person. The egoistical person is like the narcissistic not able really to love. He too is not very much interested in the world outside and wants everything for himself, but the very egotistical person may have a very good concept of the world outside.

The vain person, at least a certain kind of *vanity*, is usually not a particularly narcissistic person. He is usually a very insecure person who needs confirmation all the time. So he will ask you if you like him; if he is clever and psychoanalytically trained he will not do so outright but in a slightly indirect way. But actually what he is principally concerned with is—to be concerned with his own sense of insecurity, but that is not necessarily narcissistic.

The *truly narcissistic person* doesn't give a damn what you think about him because there is no doubt that what he thinks about himself is real and that every word he says is just wonderful. And if you meet a really narcissistic person, and if he comes into a room and says: "Good morning" then he feels, "Isn't that wonderful." He is just there and says good morning. It's something beautiful for him.

The result of narcissism is the *distortion of objectiveness* and judgment because for the narcissistic person, "that is good which is mine and that is bad which is not mine." The second result is the *lack of love* because obviously I do not love anybody outside if I only am concerned with myself. Freud has made a very significant remark here. Many relationships seem like love, namely relationships with children and among people who are what they call in love with each other. Actually this kind of relationship very often is only a narcissistic one. That is to say, in a mother's love of her children, she actually loves herself because they are her children.

I would not say that this is necessarily so, but this is indeed very frequent and therefore very often the narcissistic character of such a person is hidden behind appearances, which are those of a loving attitude toward another person.

Another result is that if narcissism is *disappointed* within a person, then you have two reactions: one of anxious *depression,* and one of rage. That depends on many factors. I would say, just as a footnote, that I think it is a very interesting problem psychiatrically to study to what extent psychotic depressions are the result of severe wounds to narcissism—that the mourning of which Freud speaks as part of the depression is not the mourning over the image of the narcissistic ego that has been destroyed rather than the mourning over another person that has been incorporated. In regard to the reaction of *rage:* If you hurt the narcissistic person's feelings, you find a great deal of rage. Whether that rage is conscious or not depends mainly on the social position. If he has power, then probably his rage will be quite conscious. If you have power over him, he will not dare to have conscious rage, and you will find a depressed person. But maybe, once, if the situation changes, you will find a rage rather than a depression.

The Pathology of Normalcy, pp. 115–17.

[In contrast to narcissism experience in the being mode of existence] means that I experience myself as the true center of my world, as the true originator of my acts. This is what it means to be original.

Perhaps I can explain it best by mentioning a concrete example. A woman who has been preparing peas in the kitchen enthusiastically tells a friend whom she sees later in the morning: "I experienced something wonderful this morning; I saw for the first time that peas roll." Many people, on hearing this, would feel somewhat uncomfortable and begin to wonder what is the matter with the woman. They take it for granted that peas roll, and their only surprise is that somebody can be excited at it. But what they really experience in seeing peas roll is a confirmation of knowledge, rather than the full perception of rolling peas by the whole person.

It is striking to see the difference between this kind of adult behavior and the attitude of a two-year-old child toward a rolling ball. The child can throw this ball on the floor again and again and again, seeing it roll a hundred times, and never be bored. Why? If seeing a ball roll is merely a mental act confirming the knowledge that balls roll, one experience is enough. There is nothing new in the second and third and fiftieth experience. In other words, one gets bored in seeing it again and again; but for the child this is primarily not a mental experience but a delight in really seeing the ball rolling, a delight that many of us still feel when we watch a tennis game and see the ball bouncing back and forth.

If we are fully aware of a tree at which we look—not of the fact that this is correctly called a tree, but of this tree, in its full reality, in its suchness—and if we respond to the suchness of this tree with our whole person, then we have the kind of experience that is the premise for painting the tree. Whether we have the technical skill to paint what we experience is another question, but no good painting is ever done unless there is first a full awareness and responsiveness toward the particular object.

To view it from still another angle, in conceptual knowledge the tree we see has no individuality; it stands there only as an example of the genus "tree"; it is only representative of an abstraction. In full awareness there is no abstraction; the tree retains its full concreteness, and that means also its uniqueness. There is only this one tree in the world, and to this tree I relate myself, I see it, I respond to it. The tree becomes my own creation.

What we experience when we see people is not customarily different from what we experience when we see things. What goes on when we believe we see a person? We see, first of all, marginal things. The color of his skin, the way he is dressed, his social class and education, whether he is friendly or unfriendly, useful or not useful. What we want to know first is his name. The name permits us to classify him, just as we classify the flower by saying that it is a rose. The way we perceive him is not too different from the way in which he perceives himself. If we ask him who he is, his first answer will be to tell us that his name is Jones, and if we show that we do not feel fully informed about him yet, he will add that he is a married man, father of two children, and a doctor. Anyone who even then does not feel that he knows this man is obviously lacking in perspicacity, or inordinately intrusive.

We see in the concrete person an abstraction, just as he sees an abstraction in himself and in us. We do not want to see more. We share the general phobia of being too close to a person, of penetrating through the surface to his core, and so we prefer to see little, no more than is necessary for our particular dealings with him. This kind of marginal knowledge corresponds to an inner state of indifference in our feeling toward the other person.

But this is not all. We do not see the person only marginally and superficially. In many ways we also see him unrealistically. We see him unrealistically in the first place because of our projections. We are angry, project our anger at the other person, and think he is angry. We are in vain and perceive him as vain. We are afraid and perceive him as afraid. And so on. We make him the coat hanger of the many suits that we do not like to wear ourselves and are not aware that these are only the clothes that we put on him. Aside from projecting, we do a lot of distorting with the other person, because our own emotions make us incapable of seeing the other person as he is.

"The Creative Attitude," p. 50 and pp. 45–46.

Idolatry (as a Compensation for Unbelief) versus Humanistic Religiousness

Man is not an empty sheet of paper upon which culture and society write their script, but man is born with certain necessities already latent in his existence. One example for such existential needs is the fact that every person must have a system of orientation and devotion. Man must have a view of the world according to which he orients himself. It does not matter very much whether the view is right or wrong. However the view might seem, he needs it, because otherwise he could not act. This is a basic point of human existence that is not true of animals. An animal does not have to search out its own path; an animal is already predetermined to act in the right manner; in this respect, it has no problems.

Man needs a frame of orientation and an object of devotion. Even if he has at his disposal all kinds of material and sexual gratification, he is still not happy with that and is not even safe from insanity. This could be shown by many examples. Many young people from rich families have everything—girls, cars, etc.—and yet many of them are miserable, unhappy human beings who do not know what they should do with their lives, who drink, take drugs, and race around from one pleasure to the other.

In America, interesting experiments were conducted with people who were deprived of sensory stimuli. They were taken to a room in which they heard nothing and were subject to no stimuli whatsoever, although they were well provided for materially. They did not have to do anything, were paid very well, and actually should have felt very well. Yet, after a very short time, these people showed symptoms of severe psychological disturbances.

Interview with Reif 1974, pp. 59–60.

When I speak here of the psychological problems of surplus society, I mean what people usually call *religious problems* and what I personally would prefer to call by the term *X problems,* because that is a symbol that has no specific historical reference.

"Problems of Surplus," p. 317.

"Religion" as I use it here does not refer to a system that has necessarily to do with a concept of God or with idols or even to a system perceived as religion, but to *any group-shared system of thought and action that offers the individual a frame of orientation and an object of devotion.* Indeed, in this broad sense of the word no culture of the past or present, and it seems no culture in the future, can be considered as not having religion.

This definition of "religion" does not tell us anything about its specific content. People may worship animals, trees, idols of gold or stone, an invisible god, a saintly person, or a diabolic leader; they may worship their ancestors, their nation, their class or party, money or success. Their religion may be conducive to the development of destructiveness or of love, of domination, or of solidarity; it may further their power of reason or paralyze it. They may be aware of their system as being a religious one, different from those of the secular realm, or they may think that they have no religion, and interpret their devotion to certain allegedly secular aims, such as power, money, or success, as nothing but their concern for the practical and the expedient. The question is not one of *religion or not?* but of *which kind of religion?*—whether it is one that furthers human development, the unfolding of specifically human powers, or one that paralyzes human growth.

To Have Or to Be?, p. 135.

The spirit of capitalism has reduced the religious content of Marxism and of the Church to a minimum. On the other hand, there are millions of men, especially young people, who in the midst of "progress" sense the emptiness and deceptiveness of life. They ask: Who am I? Has life got a meaning, and if so, what is it? What can I plan or do in order to escape from the meaninglessness, boredom and despair that result from the fact that I have no center?

These are genuine questions. They are not invented and do not form part of an ideology. They are spoken out of a profound despair. Most of those who pose these questions now hardly believe that there is any answer to them. Others try to escape despair by reverting to primitive forms of religion; the ritual intoxication, sexual orgy, sadistic perversion, and even "neo-Satanism." Others seek "religion" and "inner liberation." Unfortunately they often fall into the hands of charlatans, whether imported or domestic, who offer for sale the religious ideas of the Orient, often mixed with Freud and "sexual liberation." Young people haven't seen anything better and therefore confuse the genuine with the fake.   "Religion and Religiousness," p. 152.

Without a map of our natural and social world—a picture of the world and of one's place in it that is structured and has inner cohesion—human beings would be confused and unable to act purposefully and consistently, for there would be no way of orienting oneself, of finding a fixed point that permits one to organize all the impressions that impinge upon each individual. Our world makes sense to us, and we feel certain about our ideas, through concensus with those around us. Even if the map is wrong, it fulfills its psychological function. But the map has never been entirely wrong—nor has it ever been entirely right. It has always been enough of an approximation to the explanation of phenomena to serve the purpose of living. Only to the degree that the *practice* of life is freed from its contractions and its irrationality can the map correspond to reality.

To Have Or to Be?, p. 137.

Marx said (MEGA I, 5, p. 535), "Philosophers have only interpreted the world differently. What matters is to change it." From the standpoint of "X," one would have to add, "Yes, one must change the world, but one has to go beyond philosophy as well as a change of the world. What matters is that man himself becomes different! But that means that man must discover values that can become efficient motives of his actions. At issue is not only the changing of the world and certainly not only the various interpretations of the world, but rather the question, 'How can man become so profoundly transformed that the values that he has hitherto recognized only ideologically, become compelling motives for his personality and his action?'"

From the "X standpoint," one must say that, at the moment of his birth, man is confronted with a question that he must answer during every moment of his life, namely, the question of what it means to be a human being. The "non-X person" does not at all see this question because he is satisfied with what consumption offers him or—what is rare today—because he is content to act in the sense of morals. The X-person, on the other hand, gives an answer to this question, and this answer is not primarily an intellectual answer, but rather an answer of his total personality.

"Problems of Surplus," pp. 326–27.

[Faith in the being mode of existence] means to consider the whole process of life as a process of birth, and not to take any stage of life as a final stage. Most people die before they are fully born. Creativeness means to be born before one dies.

The willingness to be born requires *courage* and *faith*. Courage to let go of certainties; courage to be different and to stand isolation; courage, as the Bible puts it in the story of Abraham, to leave one's own land and family and to go to a land yet unknown. Courage to be concerned with nothing but the truth, the truth not only in thought but in one's feelings as well.

This courage is possible only on the basis of *faith*. Faith not in the sense in which the word is often used today, as a belief in some idea that cannot be proved scientifically or rationally, but faith in the meaning that it has in the Old Testament, where the word for faith *(Emunah)* means certainty; to be certain of the reality of one's own experience in thought and in feeling, to be able to trust it, to rely on it, this is faith.   "The Creative Attitude," pp. 53–54

[Faith in the being mode of existence does not mean the wish to become God but to become fully human.] The idolization of man is actually what has happened in the development of modern industrialism and with increasing rapidity in the last decades. By knowing the secrets of nature man feels that he becomes omniscient and by controlling nature he becomes omnipotent. The creation of nature by God is followed by the creation of a *second* nature by man. The denial of God is followed by the elevation of man into the role of God. This process was not conscious as such; it could not be conscious because morality on which bourgeois society was built was still embedded in religious concepts. Indeed, as Dostoyevsky already recognized, if God is dead, everything would be allowed!

What would happen to civil society if everything was allowed? The traditional religious cover had to be preserved in order to guarantee the effectiveness of concepts such as duty, loyalty, patriotism, respect for law. Underneath this conscious cover, however, man was fired and sustained by the new vision of himself as god. This new paganism in which man became an idol contains the deepest psychological motivation for the energy and skill that were necessary to construct the world of modern technique. Driven by this vision, or if you like, drunk with it, man performed the miracles of technique that man dreamed of, or even did not dream of, in his previous history. Has space travel not made him the creature of the universe, eliminating the limitations of space? Has he not acquired the possibility of changing the structure of the brain and altering reactions that seemed to be fixed by God's creation? Are not the secret services (CIA, KGB) that can photograph and listen in to the most private happenings as omniscient as one once believed God to be?

Indeed man is on the way to becoming God—or so he thinks—and this is his answer to the religious tradition and the basis for complete negation of ethics. Yet in order to become God, man has to become inhuman—and thus in the long run destroy himself by sacrificing himself at the altar of the true God to whom the Man-God has to abdicate eventually—*technique.*   *On Being Human,* pp. 168–69.

The deification of man in the works of his own hand leads to man's becoming reduced to such a passive, empty, alienated *homo consumens* that he loses all of his inner animation. In reality, the question today is not whether God is dead, but whether man is dead. "Problems of Surplus," pp. 327.

It seems to me that the common concern of Christian as of non-Christian religiousness is to speak about the essential part of the "religious tendency," as it can be described in a language understood by those who suffer under their alienation; about the minimum requirements in regard to patience, self-discipline, and practice if one is just to take the first steps; and about how one is to distinguish the genuine from the false, truth from deception, and not judge another human directly, according to *what* he says, but according to *how he is.* "Religion and Religiousness," pp. 152–53.

The dialogue between religious theists and religious nontheists is in the somewhat difficult position of not having a suitable language because, for 2,000 years, all concepts have been oriented toward western religions, especially toward Christianity. That is why, for example, the study of Buddhism is of such great interest: it is a religion that is nontheistic, that knows no god, and that nevertheless essentially accords very closely with Christian and Jewish mysticism. The comparison of a mystic like Meister Eckhart with certain Buddhist texts evinces a nearly complete agreement. Indeed, I believe that there is no disagreement between theistic-religious people and nontheistic-religious people, that there should be no disagreement, and that both should act according to the principle of understanding the other person points, one should, on the contrary, first see one's own weak points.

Of course, both religious traditions, the theistic and the nontheistic, have points in their development and their thought about which one can argue. Yet both groups have essentially the same basic position that is nevertheless incompatible with the position of idolatry, which is the position of the great majority within as well as outside religion. Idols are unliving things; they are the work of man's hands, and man bows before his own work. He takes a piece of wood; with one piece, he makes a fire to bake his cake, and with the other piece he makes an idol to which he prays. The concept of alienation has perhaps been nowhere so profoundly portrayed as in the literature of the Prophets.   "Problems of Surplus," pp. 327–28.

The service of idols is the reification and alienation of the living man. God is the nameless and living. Idols are dead things, and those who pray to them become dead things. Idolatry is the self-denial of man as a living being. The idols of modern, greedy, alienated man are production, consumption, technology, the despoiling of nature. His belief is to expect salvation as the total conquest of nature; he believes that in the end he will himself become God: he replicates the creation—only he is better at it, being a scientist. The richer his idols, the poorer a man is. Instead of joy, the search is for satisfaction and arousal. Instead of *being,* man looks for *having* and using. Instead of the living, he chooses the dead.

Whereas "theology" is not common to radical Christians and non-Christians; they nevertheless share a conviction of what is the essence and the evil of idolatry, whether they use this term, or its synonym, "alienation." Whatever the case, "ido-logy"—the "science of idols"—is possible and necessary. "Idology" is possible because idols are things that one can make and therefore know. It is necessary because the idols do not announce themselves as such. They are no longer called Baal and Astarte, and do not belong to a specific alien "religion"; on the contrary, they bear respectable names, such as "honor" or "state sovereignty"; they are supposed to be wholly rational, like technology; objects of the striving proper to human nature, such as consumption; finally, even God himself becomes an idol in whose name all false deities are blessed.

Radical criticism of society and religion has a religious function: it is the exposure of idols and hence the condition for true religiousness. The disclosure of the idols and struggle against them form the bond that joins or (as I think) should join religious men, Christian and nontheist, together.   "Religion and Religiousness," pp. 153–54.

Denial of Death (as a Compensation of Fear of Death) versus Love of Life

It may be possible for us not to attach ourselves to *property* and, hence, not fear losing it. But what about the fear of losing life itself—the fear of dying? Is this a fear only of older people or of the sick? Or is everybody afraid of dying? Does the fact that we are bound to die permeate our whole life? Does the fear of dying grow only more intense and more conscious the closer we come to the limits of life by age or sickness?   *To Have Or to Be?*, pp. 125–26.

It is one thing that a person may not have a strong wish to live and it is quite another thing that he might be terribly frightened of dying. The fear of death is in proportion to the feeling of not having been fully alive, that is to say of having spent a life that was not particularly joyful or meaningful. The person who is fully alive is little afraid of death because his identity lies in his being and his inner activity. But those, like most in our culture whose identity lies in what they have—material possessions, social position, prestige, power, etc.—fit into the formula, "I am what I have." Their self is the sum total of what they have and the most precious possession is their ego, their person. The fear of death with them is not so much the fear of not living but the fear of the loss of the most precious thing they have, their person.

One has to consider both conscious and unconscious manifestations of being afraid of dying and of death. [Those manifestations are the denial of death, the belief in his immortality, and the necrophilous longing for death.]

Many people are very much afraid of dying and consider death—or rather their own death—a taboo subject. A case in point would be the fact that many people are afraid of making a will. Precisely for the same reason this phobic attitude is often consciously rationalized in the words of "tempting Providence." In fact one might say there is a good deal of superstition in this whole attitude. One should not mention certain terrible things because even their mention will make them happen. There are cases where people commit suicide because they are so afraid of dying.

"The Will to Live," p. 520.

[Also the longing for death can be understood as a manifestation of fear of death because of a nonlived life.] You will find many people who are most interested in burials, in death, in sickness, whose favorite conversation is the history of their sicknesses and you can see that for older people this could easily become much more of a rationalized preoccupation than for younger people.

When the necrophilous person sees that he has perhaps only ten or fifteen years to live and death becomes very close to his heart, he finds that he does not have to repress his necrophilous tendencies anymore. He can now, overtly, be concerned with sickness and death and he becomes not only a bore, but a real danger for all who live around him because he spreads an atmosphere of gloom gleefully. For him, of course, it isn't really gloom; for him, it's the most exciting thing in the world—to think about sickness and death. But for people who love life, it's terrible. Now, if you don't know that you are dealing with what you might call, in a broad sense, a sickness, then you might easily find yourself caught in this atmosphere of gloom particularly if you feel a compassion for this person who cannot stop talking about illness.

I think if one does care for the aged, one should be very aware that this preoccupation with sickness, death, and burials, is not at all just a natural outcome of being old. Most of the time it is the more frank expression or manifestation of a tendency these people have had all their lives; namely, to get excited about the one thing that one should not get excited about, and that is decay.

"Problems of Aging," p. 53.

The fact that people do not use the opportunity for medical examinations that may aid early detection of cancer or other illnesses, when in fact they could, through use of these opportunities, protect themselves from severe illness or premature death [leads to another manifestation of denying the death:] the "illusion of immortality." The individual really does not believe that he could die, and hence is not sufficiently motivated to act in order to avert the danger of death.

As is well known we camouflage death and make it unreal. The body is beautified, the burial handled by the professional "mortician," burial becomes a social occasion, and feelings of grief are greatly restrained. It seems to me that this denial of death is deeply rooted in an attitude that pervades our whole culture, and that is our estrangement from nature. Nature since the Renaissance is the object of conquest. Man's greatest pride is to conquer nature completely, to create a new man-made world, to become omniscient and omnipotent (science and technique) like God.

Death is really the one phenomenon that belies the myth of our conquest of nature. It shows the very limits of our technique and nothing is more natural than to cope with this objectionable fact by denying it—denying it of course not in a scientific sense but in an experiential sense; dying and death are, as it were, unspeakable, or perhaps to put it accurately, "unfeelable." This phenomenon of the denial of death becomes much more apparent if we compare the attitude towards death in practically all other cultures preceding our own, in which man remained part of nature rather than its conqueror.   "The Will to Live," pp. 518–19.

There is only one way—taught by the Buddha, by Jesus, by the Stoics, by Master Eckhart—to truly overcome the fear of dying, and that way is by *not hanging onto life, not experiencing life as a possession.* The fear of dying is not truly what it seems to be: the fear of stopping living. Death does not concern us, Epicurus said, "since while we are, death is not yet here; but when death is here we are no more" (Diogenes Laertius). To be sure, there can be fear of suffering and pain that may precede dying, but this fear is different from that of dying. While the fear of dying may thus seem irrational, this is not so if life is experienced as possession. The fear, then, is not of dying, but of *losing what I have:* the fear of losing my body, my ego, my possessions, and my identity; the fear of facing the abyss of nonidentity, of "being lost."

To the extent that we live in the having mode, we must fear dying. No rational explanation will take away this fear. But it may be diminished, even at the hour of death, by our reassertion of our bond to life, by a response to the love of others that may kindle our own love. Losing our fear of dying should not begin as a preparation for death, but as the continuous effort to *reduce the mode of having and to increase the mode of being.* As Spinoza says, the wise think about life, not about death.

The instruction on how to die is indeed the same as the instruction on how to live. The more we rid ourselves of the craving for possession in all its forms, particularly our egoboundness, the less strong is the fear of dying, since there is nothing to lose. *To Have Or to Be?*, pp. 126–27.

If I say life ends with death I express something that Christians or Jews, who believe in a world after life, will not agree with. However, I think they would agree with me in one thing: even if one believes in life after death it is certainly not a prepaid guided tour in a very foreign country. It is no pleasure trip, it is there only if something happens in our life *here* that makes it possible to participate in that kind of life that various religious systems describe. It doesn't really matter too much whether we do or do not believe in certain religious statements or dogmas about life after death, for it would still mean we have to take this problem of death seriously and not try to camouflage it or to run away from it. "Problems of Aging," p. 12.

Steps Toward Being

The Will for Character Changes

*A*society whose principles are acquisition, profit, and property produces a social character oriented around having, and once the dominant pattern is established, nobody wants to be an outsider, or indeed an outcast: in order to avoid this risk everybody adapts to the majority, who have in common only their mutual antagonism. As a consequence of the dominant attitude of selfishness, the leaders of our society believe that people can be motivated only by the expectation of material advantages, i.e., by rewards, and that they will not react to appeals for solidarity and sacrifice. Hence, except in times of war, these appeals are rarely made, and the chances to observe the possible results of such appeals are lost. Only a radically different socioeconomic structure and a radically different picture of human nature could show that bribery is not the only way (or the best way) to influence people.

Assuming the premise is right—that only a fundamental change in human character from a preponderance of the having mode to a predominantly being mode of existence can save us from a psychological and economic catastrophe—the question arises: is large-scale characterological change possible, and if so, how can it be brought about?

To Have Or to Be?, pp. 106–7 and 168.

The problem of how to change human character has hitherto always been only a religious and moral problem. Today, for the first time in history, there are scientists such as those of the "Club of Rome" who say, "We are not interested here in the moral and religious problem. What is important is the alternative: if you want to survive, then you must change yourselves as *humans,* that is, in the sense of giving up the structure of having, of giving up the craving for luxury, and of giving up consumerism."

Aside from moral and religious values, the *physical* survival of humanity depends on a fundamental change of our character. We still know very little about the conditions under which this will happen. Profound economic and social changes certainly play a crucial role, but they do not in themselves explain everything.

Interview with Reif 1977, pp. 62–63.

What is character? It is well known that the word "character" is used in very different ways. If one says of a person that he has character, then one means something positive, i.e., that the person in question is guided by some principles, acts in a uniform manner, and that his manner of responding is distinguished primarily by stability. Of course, certain moral ideas make their way into this interpretation, since nobody would want to characterize a criminal who committed his criminal acts with a considerable amount of stability as "having character" in the sense stated above.

The word *character,* as I am using it here, has a different meaning that derives from psychoanalysis and was specifically used by Freud for the first time, although one can read character descriptions in Balzac and Dostoyevsky that even surpass those of Freud and that, considered theoretically, have exactly the same meaning. By "character," one means a system of aspirations that forms in a person at a certain point of time in his life and that, while not entirely immutable, nevertheless changes little once it has been formed. It determines how a person acts, how he feels, and how he thinks.

Now, Freud showed for the first time in a systematized fashion that man's character is a system of energies that works in quite a definite direction. That means that vital human energy is not something without form, it does not exist in a general sense, but rather always has a direction, a particular quality. In the case of the anal character, for example, it is directed toward the goal of hoarding, of saving, and of holding in reserve. Incidentally, it is by no means limited solely to purely material things. There are also sufficiently many people with a markedly anal, i.e., stingy, character. Yet their stinginess is primarily related to the psychological. There are people who are stingy with their feelings, words, gestures and who are unconnected, cold, and "ungiving" in their entire being.

Interview with Reif 1974, pp. 33–34; 37–38.

When questioning the significance of character, the issue is not only about an individual character and the question of who I am and who others are, but rather it is primarily about what I have called the "social character." I need to explain this somewhat more fully, since it is quite essential for the concept of character as well as for the concept of the motivation of the individual.

Man is essentially distinguished from animals by the fact that his actions barely continue to be compromised by instincts. When I say that man is distinguished from animals, then I must add that, in the evolution of man, instinctual determination becomes weaker and weaker the more we ascend up to the primates. In the case of man himself, it is extraordinarily minimal. Of course, there are some instinctual things, but they are already very much intertwined with factors of learning and environment: hunger, thirst, the need to sleep, aggression as defensive aggression, sexuality to a certain degree, and perhaps what people call motherly love, but that is already quite questionable. You cannot live from that!

A person who is driven by these impulses does not know how he should stay alive in a given society. Seen in this way, man would be the most helpless of all animals and would not at all know what he should do and how he should behave. Thus, he needs a substitute for lacking instincts; to a certain degree, he needs a "second nature." He needs something that enables him to act under given circumstances without hesitating and without reflecting. This is made possible by character.

In contrast to character, which is dependent upon environmental conditions, one speaks of instinct if a quite definite manner of reacting is built into the brain, a manner that, while not entirely independent of external circumstances, nevertheless functions essentially autonomously, reacts by itself, and leads to certain impulses. Sexuality is one example. One can say of it that it is an instinct. One cannot say of it that sexual desires are present in one group of people but simple are not present in another. Sexuality is simply present and is heightened or made manifest in individual cases by certain objects. If these objects are not present, then sexual desires and fantasies are nevertheless present.

Marx distinguishes general, fixed urges, such as hunger and sexuality, from those urges that are determined socially, such as greed. Greed develops in certain social classes, in others not. To a certain extent, my theory of social character follows the Marxist division between fixed and relative drives, except that, by introducing the concept of character, I am speaking here not of individual urges, but rather of character structure.

Character is the substitute, the replacement of instinct under human conditions in which instinct as a neurophysiologically and biologically given factor is as yet developed only very slightly. But how does character develop?

In a historical-biological sense, the character of people develops in such a way that, in a particular society, they *want* to do what they *must* do, that is, they are driven to think, to behave, and to react in *such* a way as is necessary for the preservation of the society as a whole—and not only for the preservation of the species—under the given social circumstances. For example, a person in a society of warriors must have a warlike, aggressive character. He must like to go on campaigns, he must enjoy fighting and killing, etc. Yet the same person would be quite unsuited in a society of cooperative farmers; he would hardly be able to exist there, since there is no place for these qualities in such a society. There, he must have a character that motivates him to cooperate, to maintain friendly relations with others and to share with them.

"Modern" man, man in a cybernetic society, for whom marketing character is typical, is driven to submit himself to an anonymous authority, to do what the organization wants, to have no feelings, to achieve, to develop enough ambition in order to make progress, but only just as much as is in accord with social demands; for others, on the other hand, this means that they must be content with what they have. Every society produces the character that it needs.

Now, society does not exist in a general sense. There are only *specific societies*. As a result, there are also only specific human structures of energy, not man in the sense that energy is structured and formed in a certain manner. Seen from the standpoint of society, all institutions—upbringing, school, advertisement, newspapers, etc.—work to produce this character in every aspect. Or to put it differently: society cannot use human energies, which are one of the primary productive forces as *energy in general*. It must convert this energy into a *specific energy* that is necessary for its social purposes. In the case of social character, then, the issue is the transformation of general energy into specific energy that is required by society within a particular social system and that society wants to generate.

Of course, an understanding of character has extraordinary importance in practical life. People get taken in by other people so often because they only see their behavior and not their character. What would happen if people in a democracy were to recognize the character of a political leader instead of being taken in by his speeches or his gestures? The words are totally uninteresting! One knows much more about a person when one looks *at* his mouth than when one listens to what he says *with* his mouth.

Characterology is concerned with discerning how one recognizes a person's character. These are often small details. It usually does not matter what a person thinks or says. The person himself might or might not be convinced of his more or less great ideas; even if he is convinced of them, they are usually just words. What difference would it make not only in politics, but also for the problem of love and marriage if one could duly recognize character? People fall in love with one another or believe that they love one another because they do not correctly evaluate their characters. After ten years, they find out why they cannot live together. But it would have been possible for them to determine this after just three weeks if they had taken the trouble to understand the other person's character.

When I speak here of social character as a character that is necessary and useful for a given society, that does not mean that society succeeds in producing this character in all people. Because of individual or constitutional factors, there are always people who are not in harmony with the character of a society. There would be no historical development whatsoever if there were not people in every society who, because of the fact that they are not in harmony with the social character, were in a position to have a transfigurative and revolutionary effect on society.

There can be individual reasons why such characters come to be, resulting from quite specific events within the family. Constitutional factors can also play a role; but it can also be that these characters developed exactly because they did not derive from the mainstream of society. The revolutionary leaders of 1917, for example, were predominantly people who had come from the middle or upper class; this is also true of the Russian Decembrists. In contrast, some of them were not exactly the most dependable people. This means that education, the influence of ideas from the wide world, the influence of world literature, of philosophy, and of everything that was accessible to them, plus certain familial and personal characteristics—one needs only to think of Marx himself here—led [to the fact] that their character was not in harmony with the average character of the society of the time and that, for that reason, they could become leaders who wanted to change conditions in a way that no longer corresponded to the traditional social character. These exceptions are not merely given facts; they are also tremendously important historically, because they present mutations that make social changes possible when the general political and social conditions of such a change are favorable at the same time. If that is not the case, then these people probably remain in the margins, because no one listens to or notices them, because they are simply crazy or are thought to be crazy and sometimes even become crazy in their complete isolation.

Interview with Reif, pp. 49; 85–87;
51–53; 57–58; 64–66; 54–56.

The will to live is such a deeply rooted biological tendency in man that it expresses itself not only in his physiological being, but also in his brain. Everything in man is directed toward preserving life and advancing life. I can hardly imagine that things could come to a point where man gives us his will to live, such as during an outbreak of a general state of delirium that leads to self-destruction.

Interview with Jaenecke.

The frequency and intensity of the desire to share, to give, and to sacrifice are not surprising if we consider the conditions of existence of the human species. What is surprising is that this need could be so repressed as to make acts of selfishness the rule in industrial (and many other) societies and acts of solidarity the exception.

To Have Or to Be?, p. 106.

Violence as such never creates anything new. Novelty must already be present. Most of all, the forms of society that stand in the way of love must be replaced by ones that promote it. There is still the hope that people will recognize their own suffering that is brought about by a lack of love. Out of this suffering, new and strong drives will emerge toward love and thus toward life as well.

A change is possible only if the majority of people one day see that things cannot continue as they are; we are giving ourselves up to illusions. We are not happy with everything that we spend, with our entire lifestyle; nor are

children happy. It is not impossible that there will be then people who will proclaim this truth in a convincing way.
Interview with Jaenecke.

My personal estimate is that the young people (and some older ones) who are seriously concerned with changing from the having to the being mode number more than a few dispersed individuals. I believe that quite a large number of groups and individuals are moving in the direction of being, that they represent a new trend transcending the having orientation of the majority, and that they are of historical significance. It will not be the first time in history that a minority indicates the course that historical development will take. The existence of this minority gives hope for the general change in attitude from having to being.

This hope is all the more real since some of the factors that made it possible for these new attitudes to emerge are historical changes that can hardly be reversed: the breakdown of patriarchal supremacy over women and of parents' domination of the young. While the political revolution of the twentieth century, the Russian Revolution, has failed, the victorious revolutions of our century, even though they are only in their first stages, are the women's, the children's, and the sexual revolutions. Their principles have already been accepted by the consciousness of a great many individuals, and every day the old ideologies become more ridiculous. *To Have Or to Be?*, p. 76.

Changes of Practice of Life

One can state as a rule that there is no period in the past that can serve us as a model, since every epoch is confronted with new problems. If the question is put in a more general way, then, indeed, I do think that the thirteenth century, for example, was in many regards an epoch of history with which we could again become acquainted, even though it could not be a model for us. In the thirteenth century—and this has been clearly shown by the historian Carl L. Becker (1932)—western Europe began to develop a relatively undogmatic religious attitude, to a large extent in the form of a radical humanism; at the same time, there was a tremendous explosion of rational thought.

Today, rational thought has become instrumental thought. Reason has been degraded to manipulative intelligence; religious faith, like all feeling, has disappeared and has given way to a type of general schizophrenia in which the brain, and no longer the heart, is active. During the thirteenth century, but also during the fourteenth and fifteenth centuries, the world was not yet torn between reason and faith. Quite to the contrary. A synthesis had begun to develop. But this was then destroyed by the development of modern industry; more and more, man ceased to be the most important thing in life, and economics, and concommitantly machines, profit and capital, took his place. Consumption has become the de facto goal—in a broad sense one can even say the "religious" goal—of modern man while he consciously continues to believe that he is a Christian.

For certain societies that people today like to call primitive, the dominating trait of life was not the economy—this is even true of the Middle Ages—but rather man's development. Medieval culture was in fact a religious culture. This was the only time in which Europe became Christianized and, in a true sense, was converted and where this Christianity was simultaneously a humanistic Christianity. It had previously been pagan, and since the beginning of the industrial age, it has become pagan again.

Interview with Reif 1977, pp. 5–7.

If we do not want the history of humankind to end in a global catastrophe, then we must develop a form of society where, although not without technology, *man again becomes the measure of all things,* where people matter, not consumers, where what matters is the understanding of people, not the knowledge of how he best functions. This does indeed look purely utopic, and perhaps it is. But if we do not want to end up in catastrophe, then man must again become the measure of all things.

In a newly organized world that is centered around man, certain branches of handiwork could even be revitalized. By this, I am not calling for a restoration of craftsmenship, but just saying that people do things because they are important—because they are important for man, instead of man's being a small appendage of a machine. Today, we are seeing for the first time that nature has a limit and that man's behavior toward nature must change. Nature is not a foe of man that must be conquered.

Interview with Lechleitner.

If people are serious about economic changes, then there will be many ways to go about making them. Only one example is the question of the connection of centralization and decentralization. On the one hand, there are anarchistic tendencies that want to do away with all regulation. On the other hand, a majority maintains that our entire economic life would be completely impossible without centralization. Both positions are dogmas. In reality, our society—if it wants to survive—is confronted with the problem of how to combine an optimum of decentralization with a minimum of centralization. This question can be examined theoretically and empirically by the use of models. If people were to spend more time on this, then the result would be that general awareness would already change in the course of dealing with this question.

Today's social sciences are really concerned only to quite a minimal degree with the basic problems of our society. They proceed from the assumption that society is simply as it is. They hardly ask, "How is a better society possible?" And when suggestions for improvement are made, then the reaction is usually, "Sure, but that just isn't possible!" This is just as if one had told someone a hundred years ago that people could go to the moon. That person would also have said, "That's totally impossible!" Yet if one had insisted on it, then he would have been called crazy.

Interview with Reif 1977, pp. 49–51.

If the economic and political spheres of society are to be subordinated to human development, *the model of the new society must be determined by the requirements of the unalienated, being-oriented individual.* This means that human beings neither live in inhuman poverty—still the main problem of the majority of people—nor be forced—as are the affluent of the industrial world—to be a *Homo consumens* by the inherent laws of capitalist production, which demand continuous growth of production and, hence, enforce growing consumption. If human beings are ever to become free and to cease feeding industry by pathological consumption, a radical change in the economic system is necessary: *we must put an end to the present situation where a healthy economy is possible only at the price of unhealthy human beings.* The task is to construct a healthy economy for healthy people.

- The first crucial step toward this goal is that production shall be directed for the sake of "sane consumption."
- Sane consumption is possible only if we can drastically curb the right of the stockholders and management of

big enterprises to determine their production solely on the basis of profit and expansion.

• To achieve a society based on being, all people must actively participate in their economic function and as citizens. Hence, our liberation from the having mode of existence is possible only through the full realization of industrial and political participatory democracy.

• Active participation in political life requires maximum decentralization throughout industry and politics.

• Active and responsible participation further requires that humanistic management replace bureaucratic management.

• All brainwashing methods in industrial and political advertising must be prohibited.

• The gap between the rich and the poor nations must be closed.

• Many of the evils of present-day capitalist and communist societies would disappear with the introduction of a guaranteed yearly income.

• Women must be liberated from patriarchal domination.

• A Supreme Cultural Council, charged with the task of advising the government, the politicians, and the citizens in all matters in which knowledge is necessary, and should be stabilized.

• A system of effective dissemination of effective information must also be stabilized.

• Scientific research must be separated from application in industry and defense.

• An indispensable condition of a new society is atomic disarmament.

The chances for necessary human and social changes remain slim. Our only hope lies in the energizing attraction of a new vision. To propose this or that reform that does not change the system is useless in the long run because it does not carry with it the impelling force of a strong motivation. The "utopian" goal is more realistic than the "realism" of today's leaders. The realization of the new society and new man is possible only if the old motivations of profit, power, and intellect are replaced by new ones: being, sharing, understanding; if the marketing character is replaced by the productive, loving character; if cybernetic religion is replaced by a new radical-humanistic spirit.

To Have Or to Be?, pp. 176–201 passim.

Transformation of Humankind

To change the having oriented character *four preconditions* must be fulfilled:

(1) The first condition for overcoming the having orientation lies in the *capacity of being aware of it.* This is an easier task than the awareness of one's narcissism, because one's judgment is much less distorted, one can recognize facts more easily, and because it is less easy to hide. Of course, recognition of one's egocentricity is a necessary condition of overcoming it, but by no means a sufficient one.

(2) The second step to take is gaining an *awareness of the roots* of the having orientation, such as one's sense of powerlessness, one's fear of life, one's fear of the uncertain, one's distrust of people, and the many other subtle roots that have grown together so thickly that it often is impossible to uproot them.

(3) Awareness of these roots is not a sufficient condition, either. It must be accompanied by *changes in practice,* first of all by loosening the grip that the having orientation has over one by beginning to let go. One must give up something, share, and go through the anxiety that these first

little steps engender. One will discover, then, the fear of losing oneself that develops if one contemplates losing things, which functions as a prop for one's sense of self.

(4) This implies not only *giving up* some possessions, but, even more important, *habits,* accustomed thoughts, identification with one's status, even phrases one is accustomed to hold on to, as well as the image that others may have of oneself (or that one hopes he has and tries to produce); in brief, if one tries to change routinized behavior in all spheres of life from breakfast routine to sex routine. In the process of trying to do so, anxieties are mobilized, and by not yielding to them confidence grows that the seemingly impossible can be done—and adventurousness grows.

This process must be accompanied by attempting to go out of oneself and to turn to others. This means something very simple, if we put it into words. One way of describing it is that our attention is drawn to others, to the world of nature, of ideas, of art, of social and political events. We become "interested" in the world outside of our ego in the literal meaning of interest. If a person has the will and the determination to loosen the bars of his prison of narcissism and selfishness, when he has the courage to tolerate the intermittent anxiety, he experiences the first glimpses of joy and strength that he sometimes attains. And only then a decisive new factor enters into the dynamics of the process. This new experience becomes the decisive motivation for going ahead and following the path he has charted. Until then, his own dissatisfaction and rational considerations of all kinds can guide him. But these considerations can carry him only for a short while. They will lose their power if a new element does not enter—experience of well-being (fleeting and small as it may be) which feels so superior to anything experienced so far that it becomes the most powerful motivation for further progress—one that becomes stronger in and of itself the further progress goes on.

To sum up once more: Awareness, will, practice, tolerance of fear and of new experience are all necessary if transformation of the individual is to succeed. At a certain point the energy and direction of inner forces have changed to the point where an individual's sense of identity has changed, too. In the property mode of existence the motto is: "I *am* what I *have*." After the breakthrough it is "I am what I do" (in the sense of unalienated activity); or simply, "I am what I am."   *The Art of Being*, pp. 119–20.

[There are many possibilities to discover and practice one's own human forces to experience the being mode of existence. Three will be shown: (1) The Unconscious as a source of the being mode. (2) The dream understanding as a means for self-knowledge. (3) Tenderness as an example for a being oriented human passion. More "Steps to Being" are described in *The Art of Being* (E. Fromm, 1989a).]

(1) Psychoanalysis is a method which aims at the *uncovering of the unconscious*. It expects that by penetrating through the defenses and resistances of conscious thought, the unconscious reality behind the screen of consciousness can be reached; it expects, furthermore, that in the process of making the unconscious conscious, neurotic symptoms and character traits can be cured. Without entering into a discussion of the theory of neuroses and their cure, we can ask ourselves: what is the process of becoming aware of the unconscious?

Let me say first that properly speaking there is no such thing as "the unconscious." The fact is that there are experiences inside ourselves of which we are aware and others of which we are not. Freud believed, as did Spinoza and

Nietzsche before him, that *most of what is real is not conscious, and most of what we are conscious of is not real, is fiction and cliché.*

Why is that so? Man always lives in a specific kind of society; it may be a society of headhunters and aggressive warriors, of peacefully cooperating peasants, of feudal serfs and artisans, or of modern industrial workers and employees; he must live in a society if he wants to live at all, and every society must form and mold the energies of man in such a way that he *wants to do what he has to do;* the necessities of societies become transformed into personal needs, into "the social character." Concretely speaking, in a society of warriors the individual must *want* to attack and rob; in a society of peaceful peasants he must *want* to cooperate and to share; in modern industrial society he must *want* to work, to have discipline, he must be ambitious and aggressive, he must want to spend and consume (in the nineteenth century, to save and to hoard). But society forms the social character not only by stimulating certain strivings and drives, but also by repressing those tendencies that are at odds with the social patterns. To give an example: among a tribe of warriors there will be a few individuals who dislike robbing and killing. But, almost certainly, they will not be *aware* of their feeling of dislike. They might on the day of an attack against a neighboring tribe develop a psychosomatic symptom like vomiting, or paralysis of an arm; their body will express their dislike, but their conscious mind will not be aware of it.

This repression operates not only with regard to certain socially taboo strivings, but particularly with regard to one basic fact: in all societies in which there is conflict between the human interests of all individuals and the social interest of the existing society (and its elite), the society will see to it that the majority of the people do not become aware of this discrepancy. The greater the discrepancy between the specific interests of the survival of a given social order and the human interest of all its members, the more must a society be conducive to repression. Only when social interests of society and the human interest of the individual are identical will the need for repression disappear.

But why, we must ask ourselves, is man so ready to repress what he feels and thinks and experiences? Freud thinks that the reason lies in the fear of the father and of his castration threat. I believe the fear is deeper and of social nature: man is afraid of nothing more than of being ostracized, isolated, alone. In fact, utter and complete isolation is equivalent to insanity. If a society lays down the law that certain experiences and thoughts must not be felt or thought consciously, the average individual will follow this order because of the threat of ostracism that it implies if he does not.

Formally speaking, then, what is unconscious and what is conscious depends (aside from the individual, family-conditioned elements and the influence of humanistic conscience) on the structure of society and on the patterns of feelings and thoughts it produces. As to the *contents of the unconscious,* no generalization is possible. But one statement can be made: the unconscious is the whole man—minus that part of man that corresponds to his society. Consciousness represents social man, the accidental limitations set by the historical situation into which an individual is thrown. Unconsciousness represents universal man, the whole man, rooted in the cosmos: it represents the plant in him, the animal in him, the spirit in him; it represents the past back to the dawn of human existence, and it represents his future to the day when man will have become fully human, and when nature will be humanized as man will be "naturalized."

To experience my unconscious means that I know myself as a human being, that I know that I carry within myself all that is human, that nothing human is alien to me, that I know and love the stranger, because I have ceased to be a stranger to myself. The experience of my unconscious is the experience of my humanity, which makes it possible for me to say to every human being "I am thou." I can understand you in all your basic qualities, in your goodness and in your evilness, and even in your craziness, precisely because all this is me, too.

"Humanism and Psychoanalysis," pp. 75–78.

For the most part, we do not repress what is bad in us, but rather refuse to see the truth that we all actually know. We basically know everything. There is much evidence for this. If one tells someone the truth to his face, then that person finds it difficult to deny it. The truth is usually accompanied by much bitterness, hate, and misrepresentations. But if one tells another person the truth about him in a friendly way, such as a psychoanalyst should do, for example, then the other person usually does not become annoyed, but rather experiences a shock, a beneficial and positive shock. Unfortunately, this is possible only in exceptional cases. If people were to see the truth, then they would have to act differently; and if they had to act differently, then they could not stay as they are and would come into conflict with society, with their drive for success, and with many, many things that are sacred to them. For that reason, it is almost necessary that, while knowing the truth, one simultaneously represses this knowledge of the truth.

Over the course of years, I have come to the firm conclusion that we do indeed repress much in us that is bad—but who is to say what is really bad. Yet what we repress the most is the truth, because it is the most dangerous thing for our entire way of living.

We repress not only what is bad, but also what is good, because it does not fit the character of society. A simple example might make this clear. A merchant, self-employed and wealthy, tends to his shop even in old age. A young girl who is going to her first ball comes into the store. She sees a dress and is thrilled. The merchant also sees that it is the right dress for the girl. The dress costs a hundred dollars, but she has only eighty. The merchant has the urge to say, "Well, dear lady, take it for eighty." He can afford it and he is happy when he makes other people happy. But he does not do it because he thinks that he will then be considered stupid, childish, or romantic, since no grown man does such a thing.

It would be true love that would motivate him not to make this twenty-dollar profit. And he could be happy by granting this girl her favorite wish. He suppresses both because society says that a rational person does not act that way. Then, the following night, he dreams that he runs over the girl with his car and she dies. Of course, the dream magnifies things tremendously, but it shows his deep feeling of guilt because he was actually horrible toward this girl. He did not dare do something a little out of the ordinary, namely, give away the dress without a profit.

One source of the feelings of guilt that we carry around lies in the fact that we repress not only the bad, but also the best within us because it does not fit in with socially accepted norms. We live in a society that is directed toward success and profit and not in one that is founded on love. Thus, the person who acts out of a sense of love excludes himself from social thinking; he becomes an outsider. The merchant in our example can hardly tell his wife about this because she would call him an "idiot." Even less can he tell his colleagues about it; he would lose his credibility and be considered half feeble-minded. "The Unthinkable," pp. 28–29; 24.

(2) When we dream we speak a language that is also employed in some of the most significant documents of culture: in myths, in fairy tales and art, recently in the novels like Franz Kafka's. This language is the only universal language common to all races and all times. It is the same language in the oldest myths as in the dreams every one of us has today. Moreover, it is a language that often expresses inner experiences, wishes, fears, judgments and insights with much greater precision and fullness than our ordinary language is capable of. Yet symbolic language is a forgotten language, considered by most as nonsensical or unimportant. This ignorance not only prevents us from understanding the wisdom expressed in myths but also from being in touch with a significant part of ourselves. "Dreams that are not understood are like letters that are not opened," says the Talmud, and this statement is undeniably true.

There can be no doubt that many dreams express the fulfillment of irrational, asocial, and immoral wishes that we repress successfully during the waking state. When we are asleep and incapable of action it becomes safe to indulge in hallucinatory satisfaction of our lowest impulses. But the influence of culture is by no means as one-sidedly beneficial as Freud assumed. We are often more intelligent, wiser and more moral in our sleep than in our waking life. The reason for this is the ambiguous character of our social reality. In mastering this reality we develop our faculties of observation, intelligence, and reason; but we are also stultified by incessant propaganda, threats, ideologies, and cultural "noise" that paralyze some of our most precious intellectual and moral functions. In fact, so much of what we think and feel is in response to these hypnotic influences that one may well wonder to what extent our waking experience is "ours." In sleep, no longer exposed to the noise of culture, we become awake to what we really feel and think. The genuine self can talk; it is often more intelligent and more decent than the pseudo self which seems to be "we" when we are awake.

My conclusion, then, is that we may expect to find true insights and important value judgments expressed in our dreams, as well as immoral, irrational wishes. We may even find in them reliable predictions of the intensity and the direction of forces operating in ourselves and in others.

The answer is that in our culture people are no less ashamed of their best strivings than of their worst. Generosity is suspected as "foolish," honesty as "naive," integrity as "not practical." While one tendency within our complex culture presents these qualities as virtues, another stigmatizes them as "idealistic dreams." Consequently wishes motivated by such virtues often live an underground existence together with wishes rooted in our vices. To mistake rational wishes of the dreamer for expressions of irrational strivings makes it impossible for him to recognize positive goals he has set himself. Yet to see in every dream an ideal or profound religious symbol is just as fallacious. Whether a dream is to be understood as an expression of the rational or irrational side in ourselves can be determined only by a full investigation of the individual case—by knowing the dreamer's character, his associations with the dream elements, the problems he was concerned with before he fell asleep.

It is the peculiarity of dreams that inner experiences are expressed as if they were sensory experiences, subjective states as if they were actions dealing with external reality. This interchange between the two modes of experience is the very essence of symbols, and particularly of the dream symbol. While the body is inactive and the senses shut down, the inner experience makes use of the dormant faculties of sensory reaction.

A forceful illustration of the dream's symbolic language is the story of Jonah. God commanded the prophet to help the people of Nineveh to repent of their sin and so to save them. But Jonah is a man of stern justice rather than of mercy; he declines to feel responsible for sinners and attempts to escape from his mission. He boards a ship. A storm comes up. Jonah goes into the hold of the ship and falls into a deep sleep. The sailors believe that God sent the storm because of Jonah and they throw him into the sea. He is swallowed by a whale and stays inside the animal for several days.

The central theme of this symbolic, dreamlike story is Jonah's desire for complete seclusion and irresponsibility— a position that at first was meant to save him from his mission, but eventually is turned into an unbearable, prisonlike existence. The ship, the sleep, the ocean, the whale's belly—all are different symbols of that one state of existence. They follow each other in time and space, but they stand for growing intensity of a feeling—the feeling of seclusion and protection. Being inside the whale has brought this experience to such a final intensity that Jonah cannot stand it any longer; he turns to God again; he desires to be freed, to go on with his mission.

"The Nature of Dreams," pp. 45–47.

(3) *Tenderness* by its very nature, is something quite different from sex or hunger or thirst. You might say, psychologically speaking, that such drives as sex and hunger and thirst are characterized by a self-propelling dynamism; they become more and more intense and end in a rather sudden

climax in which satisfaction is achieved and nothing more is wanted for the moment.

Tenderness belongs to another type of striving. Tenderness is not self-propelling, it has no aim, it has no climax, it has no end. Its satisfaction is in the very act itself, in the joy of being friendly, of being warm, of considering and respecting another person, and of making this other person happy. I think tenderness is one of the most self-assertive, joyful experiences anyone can have, and human beings are generally capable of it. For such people there is nothing selfless about it, there is nothing sacrificial about it. It is only sacrificial for the person who cannot be tender.

I have an impression that we have little tenderness in our culture. How often do you find in the movies an expression of real tenderness between the sexes or between adults and children or between human beings in general? By this I do not mean to say that we do not have the capacity for tenderness, but that tenderness is discouraged in our culture. The reason for this is partly that our culture is one that is purpose-oriented. Everything has a purpose; everything has an aim and should lead somewhere; you must "get somewhere."

Our first impulse is to get somewhere. We have very little feeling for the process of living itself without getting anywhere, just living, just eating or drinking or sleeping or thinking or feeling or seeing something. If living has no purpose, we say, what good is it? Tenderness has no purpose either. Tenderness has not the physiological purpose of relief or sudden satisfaction that sex has.

Tenderness has no purpose except the enjoyment of a feeling of warmth, pleasure, and care for another person. So we discourage tenderness. People, especially men, feel uncomfortable when they show tenderness. Furthermore, the very attempt to deny differences between the sexes, the very attempt to make men and women as alike as possible, has prevented women from showing the amount of tenderness of which they are capable and which is specifically feminine.   "Man and Woman," pp. 18–19.

Once man has eaten of the Tree of Knowledge in paradise, he can no longer return to primeval unity. Being-in-the-world without breach, without the feeling of strangeness—this unity can no longer be regained. But there is the possibility that man, if he develops his reason and his capacity for love, can come to an entirely new unity with the world that is different from the primeval unity. He can come to a unity that has passed through the entire process of individualization and alienation and that, for that reason, is experienced on a new level. This new unity never allows difference to be entirely forgotten and it must be regained ever anew.   Interview with Reif 1977, pp. 37–38.

Bibliography

Bibliography

Becker, C. L., 1932: *The Heavenly City of the Eighteenth Century Philosophers*, New Haven (Yale University Press) 1932.

Fromm, E., 1947a: *Man for Himself*, New York (Rinehard and Co.) 1947.

———1964a: *The Heart of Man. Its Genius for Good and Evil*, New York (Harper and Row) 1964.

———1976a: *To Have Or to Be?*, New York (Harper and Row) 1976.

———1989a: *The Art of Being* (Posthumous Published Writings, edited by Rainer Funk, Vol. 1), New York (The Continuum Publishing Company) 1992.

———1991b: *Die Pathologie der Normalität. Zur Wissenschaft vom Menschen* [The Pathology of Normalcy] (Posthumous Published Writings, edited by Rainer Funk, Vol. 6), Weinheim/Basel (Beltz Verlag) 1991.

———1992b: *On Being Human* (Posthumous Published Writings, edited by Rainer Funk, Vol. 8), New York (The Continuum Publishing Company) 1993.

Hebb, D. O., 1955: "Drives and the C. N. pp. (Conceptual Nervous System)," in: *Psychological Revue*, Vol. 62, No. 4, pp. 243–254.

Marx, K.: *Karl Marx und Friedrich Engels, Historisch-kritische Gesamtausgabe* [The Complete Works of Marx and Engels] (= MEGA). Werke = Schriften = Briefe, im Auftrag des Marx-Engels-Lenin-Instituts Moskau, edited by V. Adoratskij, 1. Abteilung: Sämtliche Werke und Schriften mit Ausnahme des Kapital, quoted I, 1–6, Berlin 1932; —*Thesen über Feuerbach*, MEGA I, 5.

Spinoza, Baruch de: *Die Ethik*, Hamburg 1976 (Felix Meiner Verlag).

Sources and Copyrights

Interview with Lodemann: German Television Interview 1980 with Jürgen Lodemann of Südwestfunk Baden-Baden. —Copyright by The Erich Fromm Estate.

Interview with Reif 1974: German Interview 1974 with Adalbert Reif 1974. Copyright by The Erich Fromm Estate.

Interview with Reif 1977: German Interview 1977 with Adalbert Reif. Copyright by The Erich Fromm Estate.

Man and Society: Lecture given 1956 by Erich Fromm. Copyright by The Erich Fromm Estate.

Man and Woman: Lecture given in 1949 and first published in M. M. Hughes (Ed.), *The People in Your Life: Psychiatry and Personal Relations,* New York (A. A. Knopf) 1951, pp. 3–27. —Copyright by The Erich Fromm Estate.

The Moral Responsibility of Modern Man: First published in *Merrill-Palmer. Quarterly of Behavior and Development,* Detroit, Vol. 5 (1959), pp. 3–14. Copyright by The Erich Fromm Estate.

The Nature of Dreams: First published in *Scientific American,* Vol. 180 (1949), pp. 44–47. Copyright by The Erich Fromm Estate.

The Pathology of Normalcy: = E. Fromm, 1991b. —Copyright by The Erich Fromm Estate.

Problems of Surplus: German Lecture given in 1970 and published under the title "Die psychologischen und geistigen Probleme des Überflusses" in: Erich Fromm Gesamtausgabe, Vol. V, pp. 317–328. —Copyright by The Erich Fromm Estate.

Problems of Aging: Lecture first published in *Journal of Rehabilitation,* Washington (Sept./Oct. 1966), pp. 10–12 and 51–57. Copyright by The Erich Fromm Estate.

Religion and Religiousness: "Some Post-Marxian and Post-Freudian Thoughts on Religion and Religiousness," first published in *Concilium,* Nijmegen (Stichting Concilium), Vol. 8 (1972), pp. 181–191. —Copyright by The Erich Fromm Estate.

Social Character in a Mexican Village: together with Michael Maccoby, Englewood Cliffs (Prentice Hall) 1970. —Copyright by The Erich Fromm Estate and Michael MacCoby.

The Unthinkable: Transcript of a German Lecture entitled "Das Undenkbare, das Unsagbare, das Unaussprechliche," presented by Erich Fromm on a Balint meeting in March 1977 in Ascona/Switzerland. A shortened version was published in *Psychologie heute*, Weinheim (Julius Beltz Verlag), Vol. 5 (November 1978), pp. 23–31. —Copyright by The Erich Fromm Estate.

Unpublished Paper: from an unpublished introduction to Fromm's book *To Have Or to Be?* (1976a). —Copyright by The Erich Fromm Estate.

The Will to Live: First published in *Preventive Medicine*, New York (Academic Press), Vol. 5 (1976), pp. 518–521. Copyright by The Erich Fromm Estate.

The Author

ERICH FROMM, born in 1900 at Frankfurt-am-Main, studied sociology and psychoanalysis. In 1933, he emigrated as a member of the Frankfurt School to the United States, moved to Mexico in 1950, and spent his twilight years between 1974 and 1980 in Switzerland. His books *Fear of Freedom* (1941) and *The Art of Loving* (1956) made him known throughout the world as a psychoanalyst and social psychologist. The alternative of *To Have Or to Be?* is the title of the compendium, written in 1976, of his humanistic thought and engagement on behalf of man's survival in a world that is characterized by alienation.

The Editor

RAINER FUNK, born in 1943, wrote his doctoral dissertation on Fromm's thought and, as Fromm's assistant, closely watched the writing of the book *To Have Or to Be?* He is the editor of the German ten-volume *Erich Fromm Gesamtausgabe (Complete Works of Erich Fromm)* and of the eight-volume *Schriften aus dem Nachlaß (Posthumous Writings)*. Aside from his work as a psychoanalyst in his private practice in Tübingen, he controls the rights to Erich Fromm's writings and possesses the posthumous manuscripts.

Also by Erich Fromm from Continuum

The Art of Being
Foreword by Rainer Funk

This posthumous volume represents a supplement to and expansion of one of Fromm's most popular books, *To Have Or to Be?* Between 1974 and 1976, late in his life, Fromm wrote far more manuscript and chapters than were actually published in that book. A number of these chapters are contained in *The Art of Being*. They deal with the "steps toward being" that the individual can take in order to learn the Art of Being. This Art of Being— the art of functioning as a whole person—is the breakthrough that the individual makes in moving from the state of mere *having* to the state of enlightened psychological and spiritual happiness, which Fromm calls, in this special sense, *being*.

144 pages 0-8264-0673-4 $11.95 paperback

The Art of Listening
Foreword by Rainer Funk

For more than half a century, Fromm practiced psychoanalysis. Although he intended to publish on his therapeutic method, these plans were never realized in his lifetime. The posthumously published writings in this volume collectively provide welcome new information about Fromm the therapist and the way he dealt with the psychological sufferings of people of our time. For Erich Fromm, the fine art of therapy is the Art of Listenng.

"[I]nteresting comments on Freud, Reich, Groddek, et al., as well as a case presentation and dream analysis. And there is a useful bibliography."—*Library Journal*

204 pages 0-8264-0654-8 $19.95 hardcover

Marx's Concept of Man
Including Karl Marx's Economic and Philosophical Manuscripts

With more than 150,000 copies sold, this classic, provocative view of Marx stresses his humanist philosophy, challenging both the former Soviet distortions and Western ignorance of Marx's basic thinking.

"Dispassionate Marxian scholars have long known that there is an amazing world of difference between the mythical Marx and the real man. This whole subject is strikingly illuminated in *Marx's Concept of Man.*"—*Newsweek*

278 pages 0-8044-6161-9 $10.95 paperback

On Being Human
Foreword by Rainer Funk

This posthumous volume collects writings from one of Fromm's most fertile periods, the 1960s. They are based on lectures, works written for specific occasions, and manuscripts intended as books. Of especial interest is an extended essay on two very different thinkers, Meister Eckhart and Karl Marx. Among the other essays are: "Modern Man and the Future," "The Search for a Humanistic Alternative," "The Idea of a World Conference," "Remarks on Relations between the Germans and Jews," and more.

"The texts aptly and poignantly illustrate Fromm's social diagnosis of the maladies of today's Western societies and his faith in a humanist renaissance. . . . This splendid volume is a welcome addition to Fromm's published legacy. Instructive foreword by the editor; bibliography; index. A 'must' for all libraries."—*Choice*

180 pages 0-8264-0576-2 $17.95 hardcover

Available at your bookstore, or may be ordered by calling toll free: 1-800-937-5557

The Continuum Publishing Company
370 Lexington Avenue
New York, NY 10017